THE SALT LAKE LOONIE

BY BRETT MATLOCK & JESSE MATLOCK

FOREWORD BY
HAYLEY WICKENHEISER

ILLUSTRATIONS BY DWIGHT ALLOTT

CPRC PRESS   University of Regina

Printed and bound in Canada at Friesens.
The text of this book is printed on 100% post-consumer recycled paper with earth-friendly vegetable-based inks.

Cover, text and icon design: Duncan Campbell, CPRC.
Editors for the Press: Brian Mlazgar and Donna Grant, CPRC.
Interior illustrations: Dwight Allott.
Cover photo: "Skate marks on the surface of an outdoor ice rink" by Anika Salsera / CanStock Photo

Thank you to: Zach Dabrowski, Trevor McKnight, Craig Morrison, and Jacques Rodgers for their comments on stories in this volume and special thanks to Rob Vanstone.

Library and Archives Canada Cataloguing in Publication

Matlock, Brett
The Salt Lake loonie : and other stories every sports fan should know / by Brett Matlock & Jesse Matlock ; introduction by Hayley Wickenheiser ; illustrations by Dwight Allott.

ISBN 978-0-88977-239-7

1. Sports—History. 2. Sports—Miscellanea.
I. Matlock, Jesse II. Title.

GV576.M38 2011   796   C2011-904652-0

10 9 8 7 6 5 4 3 2 1

Canadian Plains Research Center Press
University of Regina
Regina, Saskatchewan, Canada, S4S 0A2
tel: (306) 585-4758   fax: (306) 585-4699
e-mail: canadian.plains@uregina.ca
web: www.cprcpress.ca

We acknowledge the financial support of the Government of Canada through the Canada Book Fund for our publishing activities.

Canadian   Patrimoine
Heritage   canadien

For our family.

CONTENTS

Foreword by Hayley Wickenheiser ix
Icon legend xi

① ONCE UPON A TIME
The Good Old Hockey Game 1
Streaking 101 5
The Marathon at Marathon 8
When Bat Met Ball 12

② THE FUNNY PAGES
Fandemonium 19
What's up, Dock? or
Please Don't Try This at Home, Kids 23
Soar like an Eagle 27
The Life and Times of the Stanley Cup 31

③ HISTORY IN THE MAKING
Oh Canada! 37
Hammerin' Hank 41
Wilt, the One-Man Show 44
"Howe" Fitting 46
Gibson's Finest 49
150-Metre Clash 53

➍ A MOMENT OF SILENCE

The Thundering Herd 61

Disaster at Le Mans 64

Uruguayan Air Force Flight 571 68

United We Stand 72

➎ HALLOWED GROUNDS

Olympia and the Ancient Olympics 79

Montreal Forum 83

Madison Square Garden 88

Wimbledon 92

Indianapolis Motor Speedway 96

➏ SUPERHUMAN FEATS

Float like a Butterfly, Sting like a Bee 103

Golden Oldie 107

His Airness 110

The Olympic Lightning Bolt 113

➐ PROS WHO CON

Father Knows Best? 119

Skating Wars 123

The Shortcut 127

8 PAVING THE WAY

"Owen"-ing the Podium 133
The Battle of the Sexes 138
Hawk 'n' Awe 142
Podium Protest 146

9 E FOR EFFORT?

"Wrong Way" Riegles 153
The "Rocket" Richard Riot 157
The Worst Approach 160

10 TRIUMPH OVER TRAGEDY

Hotter than a Pistol 167
Brothers in Arms 171
The Marathon of Hope 175

11 APPARITIONS AND SUPERSTITIONS

Obsessive Compulsive Order 183
The Curse of the Bambino 188
The Curse Reversed 192
The Salt Lake Loonie 196

About the Illustrator 200
About the Authors 201

FOREWORD
by Hayley Wickenheiser

Sport has a way of uniting people like no other, in victory and in tragedy, as players and as fans. And sport stories—from the marathon at Marathon to Salt Lake City's lucky loonie—create a framework for our history.

I have been privileged to see the sport I love from all its angles, as a player and as a fan. I remember watching the iconic Edmonton Oilers with my Dad and dreaming of my own hockey triumphs. Standing on the podium at the 2002 Olympics in Salt Lake City was the realization of that dream. When I looked out on the crowd, I knew there were other young fans watching and creating their own dreams. As the gold medal was placed around my neck, I heard the thundering applause, and I couldn't help thinking about the Canadian secret beneath the ice. I am proud of that moment and cherish the memory to this day. The 'lucky loonie' story united our sport and our countries, and it's a story that will be passed from generation to generation.

The 44 stories presented here are moments just like that, when sport becomes more than just a game. Brett and Jesse have captured the heart, the determination, the awe, the wonder and the thrill of being a fan and sharing in the glory of the game, the agony of defeat and the triumph of winning.

I hope you enjoy the moments in this book as much as I did. It is a sports journey you will never forget.

Keep your stick on the ice,

Hayley Wickenheiser 22

ICON LEGEND

The following icons are used at the beginning
of each story in this book to show what subjects
and sports the story covers.

BASEBALL

FOOTBALL

BASKETBALL

SOCCER

SUMMER SPORT

WINTER SPORT

AMATEUR

HOCKEY

OLYMPICS

FANDOM

BOXING

GOLF

TENNIS

1
ONCE UPON A TIME

THE GOOD OLD HOCKEY GAME

"He shoots ... he S-C-O-R-E-S!!!" As many a Canadian hockey fan can tell you, it was the late, great Foster Hewitt who first coined that phrase commonly associated with *Hockey Night in Canada*, the world's oldest sports-related program still on the air. Indeed, hockey coverage goes back many decades, with the first televised hockey game occurring on October 11, 1952, between the Montreal Canadiens and the Detroit Red Wings (the Canadiens won, 2-1). Some 30 years earlier, on February 8, 1923, the first recorded radio broadcast of a hockey game took place (the third period of a game between Midland and North York of the Ontario Hockey Association). In the years before television and radio, hockey fans tracked results by newspaper or even by telegraph. Indeed, on February 14, 1896, the results of the Stanley Cup challenge game between the

Montreal Victorias and the Winnipeg Victorias (that's right, both teams were named "the Victorias") were telegraphed to anxious fans in Winnipeg; Winnipeg won that match 2-0.

Yes, Canadians love their hockey, and have for more than a century. But where does the game itself come from? Did it originate in Canada? Or, like so many other sports now played in Canada, is it an import from Europe or the United States? As it turns out, that's not an easy question to answer.

The first organized game of hockey in its modern form *of which there is a record*, predates the Montreal-Winnipeg Stanley Cup match only by a decade. In 1886 a game was played between students of Queen's University and the Royal Military College of Canada on the ice of Kingston harbour, in Ontario. The players in this first game wore ducked trousers and used a set of short sticks borrowed from a company in Nova Scotia. They played with an octagonal puck cut from a lacrosse ball, believed to be the oldest rubber puck in the world. The tradition of this game lives on in the annual Carr-Harris Cup between Queen's University and the Military College, commemorating the world's oldest hockey rivalry. It was a Captain James T. Sutherland who, in 1943, discovered the reference to this game, and based on his research, the Canadian Amateur Hockey Association has ruled that Kingston, Ontario, is the birthplace of modern hockey.

Even if Kingston truly is the birthplace of hockey, the game no doubt had been developing for some time before that. For example, nine years earlier, on March 3, 1875, the

FAST FACT

The word "puck" seems to be related to the Gaelic words "puc" or "poc," which mean to poke, to punch, or to deliver a blow. P.W. Joyce, in the 1910 publication *English as we Speak it in Ireland*, elaborated this definition when he stated: "The blow given by a hurler to the ball with his caman or hurley is always called a puck."

first organized game of *indoor* hockey was played in Montreal between two nine-player teams (all nine players were on the ice at the same time, as opposed to the six-player teams of the modern game). Nova Scotia newspapers chronicle a sport called "ice hurley," thus tracing the development of the game of hockey back to the early 1800s—some *eight decades* prior to that landmark game in Kingston harbour. Along with these forerunners of our national game is the oldest team sport in North America—lacrosse—originally played by many of this continent's First Nations. Early hockey equipment was obviously derived from lacrosse equipment, so it is not surprising that the Kingston puck was cut from a lacrosse ball!

There is also evidence that another First Nations game called *tooadijik*, played by the Mi'kmaq in Atlantic Canada, might be related to hockey. *Tooadijik* was played on wide-open fields with teams of five on each side of the field attempting to reach the opposite team's goal pole before being stopped. Although *tooadijik* may seem far removed from hockey, the two sports became more similar after European contact. When European settlers arrived in North America and introduced *hurleys* (wooden sticks with small flat blades on the end used to hit or lift balls), which were adapted from the Gaelic outdoor sport of *hurling* (a hybrid between lacrosse and field hockey), *tooadijik* took on a new form. This new game required a harder surface than could be found in fields and meadows, and it did not take long for players to discover that, in winter, Canada's frozen rivers and lakes were ideal. Thus, the combination of hurleys, *tooadijik*, and ice-covered surfaces gave rise to a new North American sport—*wolchamaadijik*—that was very similar to hockey.

While it is interesting to consider whether the birthplace of ice hockey is Nova Scotia, or Montreal, or Kingston or whether the game developed out of lacrosse, *tooadijik*, hurley or *wolchamaadijik*, what really matters is that the world's fastest sport continues to entertain us through the bleakest season of the year and that fans continue to be thrilled by the words: "He shoots ... he S-C-O-R-E-S!!!"

STREAKING 101

Much like the meaning of life, streaking is a bit of a mystery. The sight of someone effectively exposing his thunder in front of 50,000+ sports fanatics (more if the event is televised) raises the obvious question: "Who in his right mind would want to madly run around a sports field and let his bayonet pierce the eyes of tens of thousands... especially if the weather is on the chilly side?" On the other hand—there is something inherently funny about someone brave enough to bear nothing more than a grin and a baby-maker as an onslaught of robust security guards, hiding their smiles, chug their way around the field and try to corral the pasty white streaker. The inevitable end of this awkward, yet highly amusing, situation is an ungraceful tackle by a wheezing security guard followed by the inebriated runner's shameless walk of fame across the field to the on-site confinement centre. Streaking has slowly made its mark as a mainstay in professional sports. At any professional sporting event there's always a chance that someone will skip over the field barriers and do the *YMCA* dance in his birthday suit. For this reason, we pay homage to the first-known "streak" at a major sporting event.

It was 1974 and England was hosting France in Twickenham before a crowd of 53,000 people. An Australian man named Michael O'Brien was in the stands with a group of mates, taking in the game and a few spirits. O'Brien, an accountant who was never known to back down from a challenge, was bet 10 pounds by an Englishman that he couldn't run across the field and touch the fence on the other side. No big deal, right? Wrong. The catch was that O'Brien had to make the dash wearing nothing more than his twig and berries. Before anyone realized what was happening, there was the Australian, burning across the field with his pasty buttocks facing one side of the crowd and the captain sailing in the wind on the other side. O'Brien made nearly the full width of the field before the Bobbies got to him. One of the Bobbies, Bruce Perry, took his helmet and placed it over O'Brien's member. Perry later quipped, "It was an extremely cold day and Michael had nothing to be proud of." Upon the spry sprinter's capture, he told the Bobbies, "My friends over there bet me I couldn't reach that fence." So, being true gentlemen, before they took O'Brien down to the station to book him, the Bobbies escorted O'Brien over to the fence, helmet-covered broomstick and all, and let him win his bet. Amazingly, the streaker didn't miss any of the game. The Bobbies got O'Brien out, dressed, and down to the police station, then filled out the appropriate forms and got him back to his seat by the time the players had taken the field for the start of the second half. Unfortunately, although O'Brien did win his 10-pound bet, he was fined the same amount for his stunt and also lost his job at a London stock-broking firm, a rather hefty price to pay for his rash act.

Nonetheless, we tip our cap to you, Michael O'Brien, for paving the way for one of the most outlandish trends in sports!

THE MARATHON
AT MARATHON

At the mention of the word "marathon," many people will automatically think of Boston or New York—major cities which annually host these gruelling races of 26 miles, 385 yards (42.195 kilometres) that only the fittest can hope to compete in, much less finish. Others will think of the marathon event in the modern Summer Olympic Games, and many probably assume that the race originated in the Olympic Games in ancient Greece.

Not so. The marathon race was never part of the ancient games. Instead, the origin of the marathon run is intrinsically tied to one of the most important conflicts in history—the Battle of Marathon, which occurred in 490 BC.

During the Greco-Persian Wars (a series of conflicts between the Persian Empire and the free city states of the Greek world), the Persians had invaded Greece, and their armies had assembled near the village of Marathon, some 40 kilometres from Athens. Facing them were the soldiers of the Athenian army, aided by a contingent from the city of Plataea. The Greek army, estimated at 10,000 men, was outnumbered more than two to one by the Persian Empire's 25,000 troops. Worried about the probable outcome of a battle when facing such unfavourable odds, the Athenian generals decided to appeal for aid from the city of Sparta, militarily the strongest of the Greek city states.

Sparta was over 240 kilometres from Athens, and Greece's landscape, then as now, was mountainous and rugged, so travelling by horseback was out of the question. The only hope of a message arriving in time would be to send it by a runner—a common practice in that pre-Industrial era. The Athenians turned to a professional runner, a man by the name of Pheidippides (also known as Philippides), to deliver their plea for military assistance.

One of the best runners in Greece, Pheidippides set off immediately, and arrived in Sparta within 24 hours (although some sources say the journey was completed within a 48-hour span). Unfortunately, his epic trek was for nothing, as the Spartan reply was unfavourable. (Spartan religious beliefs prevented their army from fighting until the moon was full.) Thus, Pheidippides once again made the gruelling trek back to Athens to relay the Spartan refusal. Upon receiving the young runner's news, the Athenians decided that their only hope of victory lay in immediately launching a surprise attack against the Persian army at Marathon. And so, 9,000 Athenians and 1,000 Plataeans marched to battle, ready to fight and die for the freedom of Greece. To the astonishment of the ancient world, the Greeks were victorious in the subsequent battle, defeating the hitherto invincible Persians.

There are two accounts of the events following the battle. The first, found in *The Histories* by the Greek historian Herodotus, states that although the Persians lost the battle at Marathon, they were yet not prepared to admit defeat. Instead, they retired to their ships and set sail for Athens, determined to carry out their own surprise counterattack on the defenceless city. However, the Athenians—who were athletes as well as soldiers—undertook a forced march from Marathon back to Athens. Despite their exhaustion following the desperate battle they had just fought, the Greeks successfully made their way over the rugged terrain back to Athens before the arrival of the Persian ships—a feat no one had thought possible, since travel by sea was generally considered to be the fastest means possible. Faced with the possibility of fighting another battle against the army that had defeated them the previous day, the Persians decided that discretion was the better part of valour, and sailed for home. According to this account of events, the epic march of the Athenian army is considered to be the origin of today's marathon.

The other account of the story gives credit for the original marathon run to the heroic Pheidippides. After their victory over the Persian army, the Athenian commanders ordered Pheidippides back to Athens to relay the good news. Despite the fact that he was already exhausted from his previous treks between Athens and Sparta, Pheidippes set off immediately. In searing temperatures of up to 39°C (102°F), Pheidippides made the run back to Athens without stopping. Upon his arrival, he was able to gasp out but a single word— "victory"—before he collapsed and died. Hence, what we now know today as a "marathon" is a tribute to the memory of the incredible run that Pheidippides made from Marathon to Athens to relay the news of the victorious battle and the salvation of Greece.

WHEN BAT MET BALL

Although baseball is widely regarded as "America's sport," surprisingly little is known about its origins. According to some sources—including a commemorative plaque at the site—the first officially recorded game of baseball was played at the Elysian Fields, in Hoboken, New York, on June 19, 1846, between the New York Knickerbockers and the New York Nine. The game was a blowout, with a final score of 23 to 1 in favour of the "Nine" (after four innings). While this might have been the first *officially* recorded game of baseball, it was most certainly not the first game that was ever played.

For a long time, the earliest reference to a game of baseball in North America was thought to be from 1823. A news article in the *National Advocate* made reference to a game by the name of "base ball" (two words) being played in lower Manhattan. However, a recent find in Pittsfield, Massachusetts, allows us to trace the origin of baseball back even further.

In 1791, a law was enacted in Pittsfield to ban baseball from being played within 80 yards of the new courthouse, in order to protect the building's windows (some things never change!). And that's the earliest reference to baseball in North America that has so far come to light.

Before that, there is only speculation, but it would appear that the modern version of baseball can trace its ancestry back to the 1700s—not to one game, but to several. These included "goal ball," "rounders," "stool ball," "trap ball," and the gentlemen's favourite, cricket. What these had in common was that all were forms of stick-and-ball games, where one player threw a ball and another swung a stick. The English game of "rounders" seems to be the closest cousin to today's game of baseball, as it employed fielding and hitting, and four bases that the hitter had to "round" without being called "out"— via a caught ball or by being hit with a ball by a fielder.

Thus, it seems that today's version of baseball is the result of immigrants bringing their games to North American shores from around the world, where the games, like the immigrants themselves, then began to intermingle. Over time and many innings of scrub baseball, the game took shape and evolved into the multi-billion dollar industry it is today.

Although General Abner Doubleday has been called the "Father of Baseball," the claim that he created the game, and its rules, in Cooperstown, New York (the home of the Baseball Hall of Fame) is unlikely, as Doubleday was nowhere near Cooperstown in 1839 (the year he supposedly invented baseball on a Cooperstown sandlot). Nor is there any mention of baseball in any of Doubleday's surviving letters and diaries. Instead, it appears that two men by the names of Alexander Cartwright and Dr. Daniel Lucius Adams are more likely to be the proper owners of the title "Fathers of Baseball"—a title they earned in 1845. Adams and Cartwright were members of the first formal baseball club, the New York Knickerbockers, the team that played at the Elysian Fields (see above). The

FAST FACT

If you're a "cat person," you might want to skip this section. You see, another possible antecedent for the modern game of baseball was a Scottish game known as "dog and cat." The "cat" was a piece of wood (an ancestor of the ball), which was thrown at a hole in the ground, while the "dog" was a stick (from which the bat descended). The defending player would use the "dog" to keep the "cat" out of the hole. Some versions had two holes, with the "cat" getting batted back and forth between the two.

two of them standardized a set of 20 rules—the so-called "Knickerbocker Rules"—for the club and the game. Each player was expected to "have the reputation of a gentleman."

The game as Cartwright and Adams defined it struck a chord, and its popularity took off. The National League was formed in 1876—the same National League that still exists in today's Major League Baseball—while the first World Series was played in 1903. And the rest, as they say, is history.

And then there was "cat-ball," played in early America, in which the ball was again referred to as a "cat." This game featured a pitcher, a catcher, a batter, and fielders, but no teams; instead, the game was something of a free-for-all. However, it did resemble modern baseball in that, after three swings and misses, the batter was "out."

Either way, the poor cat was on the receiving end of a lot of punishment. Maybe that's why a cat has (and needs!) nine lives?

2 THE FUNNY PAGES

FANDEMONIUM

Professional sports is more than sport—it's big business. And big business means promotion and marketing. Behind the scenes of the head-to-head clash of the sports teams are the machinations of the marketing team—coordinating everything from the peanut slinger to the anthem singers, from the mascot's antics to the newest idea for a game-day promotion. Of course, not every marketing idea is entirely successful—and some are absolute duds. With this in mind, let's take a brief journey through a couple of the worst and most chaotic game-day promotions in the history of sports.

Our first stop is in the mid-1970s at a major league baseball game between the Cleveland Indians and the visiting Texas Rangers. The game-day promotion was 10¢ beer night at the ballpark. And, really, what could be better? It's simple: I give you a dime, you give me a full glass of beer, and we continue this reciprocal relationship for the duration of the night. It's a win-win situation, right? The stadium is full and everybody leaves having had a great time, losing only a dollar (or so!) in the process. What a great idea! Or maybe not. Unfortunately, Cleveland Indians management neglected to take into consideration that sports fans tend to get rowdy, and drunken people tend to get twice as rowdy. Let's do the math: rowdy (sports fans) + rowdy, rowdy (drunken people) = 25,000+ rowdy, rowdy, rowdy drunken sports fans. Not too complicated a formula. Nonetheless, on June 4, 1974, at Cleveland's Municipal Stadium, the beer was flowing.

The early effects of the promotion were nothing that couldn't be dealt with: a heavy-set woman jumped into the on-deck circle, intent on displaying her god-given endowment(s) to the world—accompanied by raucous cheers; a father-son team had a rather unique "bonding" moment by mooning the players; a streaker tried to touch second base. But as the beer flowed more freely and the crowd got more rowdy, more clothes started coming off and the on-field trips became more frequent. Things really escalated in the bottom of the ninth inning, with hundreds of intoxicated fans throwing batteries, golf balls, folding chairs, and rocks. Then, one fan stormed onto the field, stole right fielder Jeff Burroughs' hat and glove, and made a getaway toward the stands. At this point Rangers manager Billy Martin had had enough. Shouting "Let's go get 'em, boys," he led his team— armed with bats—into battle against the rowdy fans. Indians manager Ken Aspromonte ordered his players to go to the support of their erstwhile foes! The bat racks in the home-team dugout emptied as the Indians players swarmed onto the field. It was not a pretty sight. Umpire Nestor Chylak was "double fouled": he received a cut to the head from a flying rock that required stitches, and to add insult to injury, he was also hit by a folding chair. Disgusted, Chylak declared the game a forfeit, even though it had been tied.

Amazingly, despite the outcome of the game, the Indians management had no plans to cancel the three remaining promotional 10¢ beer nights. Fortunately, American League president Lee MacPhail had more sense and banned the promotion.

The second stop in our journey through game-day promotion fiascos takes us to Chicago's Comiskey Park on July 12, 1979, for a doubleheader between the White Sox and the Detroit Tigers. It was Disco Demolition Night and the promotion was simple: fans were encouraged to bring their disco records down to the park to be destroyed during intermission. With the previous night's game drawing only 15,520 fans to the 52,000-seat stadium, the White Sox (who were 40–49 at the time) actually may have sucked more than disco! Who could have predicted that some 90,000 fans would show up at the gates that evening? Sometimes a promotion works too well.

The White Sox stuffed as many fans as possible into the park. When the gates were finally closed, some of those who hadn't been admitted scaled the walls to get a glimpse of disco's demise. The large crate rigged with explosives to be blown up at centre field between the two games quickly filled to the brim, and some fans were left still holding their most-hated disco albums. These were soon turned into makeshift Frisbees. As game one was played, more and more records sliced through the air.

Finally, the first game ended (in a 4–1 Detroit victory), and the big moment had come. Donning a military helmet, Steve Dahl—a local rock station disc jockey who had been fired by a disco station—led the crowd in the chant, "Disco Sucks, Disco Sucks." There was a 10-second countdown and KABOOM!!! Disco was demolished. The explosion, which was much bigger than expected, ripped a huge hole in the outfield grass. Thousands of fans stormed the field. Banners were burned to a crisp, batting cages were destroyed, bases and chunks of field were stolen. The situation was finally brought to order by Chicago police in riot gear. Tigers manager Sparky Anderson refused to let his team take the field due to safety concerns, causing American League president Lee MacPhail—who, faced with a second baseball riot in five years, must have wondered some days if his job was worth it—to forfeit the game to the Tigers due to the White Sox's failure to provide acceptable playing conditions. Take me out to the ball game, indeed!

WHAT'S UP, DOCK?

or

PLEASE DON'T TRY THIS AT HOME, KIDS

I t was June 12, 1970, and to Dock Ellis, something was amiss. First, the baseball kept changing size: sometimes it was as big as a beach ball, sometimes it was like a small dot. And then sometimes he saw the catcher, sometimes he didn't. Sometimes the gum in his mouth turned to powder, and sometimes it didn't. Sometimes he tried to stare down the batter and pitch while he was still looking at him. Although many things were unclear for the Pittsburgh Pirates pitcher that June evening, one thing was sure: he was standing on the pitcher's mound in San Diego in front of 50,000 people—and he was higher than a kite.

Two days earlier, Ellis had flown with the Pirates to San Diego to play a four-game series against the Padres. When he and his fun-loving girlfriend, Mitzi, landed, they immediately rented a car and headed to Los Angeles to visit a long-time friend. Upon arrival, Ellis and his friends lost no time in getting down to business. Business consisted of a mixture of organic and non-organic party favours: alcohol (organic), enough pot (also organic) for a Cheech and Chong movie, and a pocketful of amphetamines (non-organic), just to mix things up a bit. For the next 12 hours, they "partied hearty." When Ellis finally woke up sometime the next day, he decided that a little "hair of the dog" was just what the doctor ordered, so he popped some extra-potent Purple Haze (a variety of LSD), and let nature take its course. As far as Dock was concerned, this was the BEST road trip, EVER!! He had a vague feeling that he was forgetting something, but it couldn't be that important, could it? Dock figured it was best to just lay back and go with the flow.

At 1:00 p.m. the following afternoon, Mitzi woke Dock from his reverie with a ghastly message. He was supposed to be pitching against the Padres, in San Diego, that night! He knew he'd forgotten something! Dock now had a serious problem. The game started in less than five hours. Dock was still flying, but he wasn't going to get to San Diego that way.

Missing the game because he was high could very well have cost Dock his career, so he decided to make the best of it. He managed to catch a flight from L.A. to San Diego, arriving at 4:40 p.m. The game started at 6:05. He could still do it!

Dock didn't remember much from the time he left L.A. to the time he arrived at the stadium in San Diego, but what he did recall was taking somewhere between four and eight amphetamines in the clubhouse and a handful of Benzedrine during his bullpen session before the game—just to calm his nerves.

Briefly, it looked as though Mother Nature might step in and save Dock from himself, as it began to rain. However, at precisely 6:05 p.m., right on schedule, with the rain subsiding, the umpire took out his brush, swept off a muddy home plate, and called for the game to begin. With three up and three down, the bottom of the inning came all too quickly for Ellis as he found himself standing on the mound with his legs a little bit too wobbly. The mound seemed slippery as an eel, and to make matters worse, Dock couldn't see either the catcher or the batter, forcing his catcher to put reflective tape on his fingers so Ellis could see the signals.

By now, Dock was literally in a world of his own. Once the ball was hit back to him and he was forced to jump because it was coming too fast. Well, the game tape showed differently. In reality the ball was coming so slowly that it never managed to reach him and the third baseman had to come in and play it. At one point, Dock was sure he was pitching to Jimi Hendrix, who was batting with his guitar. In the fourth inning, Dock was convinced that Richard Nixon was the home plate umpire. In his own words, "I was psyched. I had a feeling of euphoria. I was zeroed in on the (catcher's) glove, but I didn't hit the glove too much."

But, as incredible as it seems, Dock kept pitching, and he either struck the batters out, or he walked them. He also managed to hit a couple of them. And guess what? By the ninth inning, Dock Ellis found himself pitching a no-hitter!

Folk singer Todd Snider wrote a song about the game that Dock pitched that day, and to take a line from the song, "The ball turned into a silver bullet and his arm into a gun." Ellis mowed down the final three batters to secure his place in the history books. He was—literally and figuratively—as high as he had ever been. Not being able to feel a stitch or a seam, Dock Ellis managed to pitch a no-hitter in a dream.

SOAR LIKE
AN EAGLE

The words "England" and "ski jumping" do not often come to mind simultaneously, but at the 1988 Calgary Winter Olympics, those words collided in the person of Michael ("Eddie the Eagle") Edwards, a 24-year-old from Cheltenham who captured the hearts and imaginations of Olympics fans the world over.

Although his daytime job was plastering walls, Michael Edwards also happened to be an accomplished, and indefatigable, athlete. He ranked ninth in the world in amateur speed skating—with a top speed of 106.8 miles per hour—and he held the world record for stunt jumping, having jumped 10 cars and six buses. An enthusiastic downhill skier since the age of 13, he had only narrowly missed being selected for the 1984 British Olympic team.

As the Calgary Olympics drew nearer, Michael was determined that this time he would "make the cut." It was all a question of finding the right sport. In the end, deciding to blend his twin passions for jumping cars and downhill skiing, he concluded that his best chance would come if he entered the Olympic ski jumping competition. What could be more natural? Also influencing his decision was the fact that it was unlikely that any other Brits would be competing in this category.

Michael began training in 1986, and in order to have access to snow and ski jumps (both a rare commodity in Great Britain), he decided to move to Lake Placid, New York, which, as home to both the 1932 and the 1980 Winter Olympics, had plenty of each.

Competing at an Olympic level requires time, commitment, and money. Having quit his job, Edwards now had plenty of the first two but, with no sponsorship, was sorely lacking in the third. He cut corners where he could, even making use of oversized, second-hand ski boots when practicing—wearing up to six pairs of socks at a time in order to make the boots fit. Nevertheless, he made progress, and managed not to break his neck. (Years later, he would tell Stuart Jeffries of *The Guardian* newspaper that, while it was a myth that he was scared of heights, he most definitely was scared of jumping, stating that: "There was always a chance that my next jump would be my last. A big chance.")

Edwards made his first international appearance as Britain's representative at the 1987 World Championships, where he finished 98th in a field of 98 competitors. Undaunted, he continued his training and by the time of the qualifying rounds for the Calgary Games, he was rated 55th in the world. His earlier suspicion that there would be no other British entries in the ski jumping category also proved to be true, and he became Britain's very first Olympic ski jumper.

It is uncertain where Edwards acquired the nickname "Eddie the Eagle," but when he arrived at the Calgary airport for the XV Olympiad, he was greeted by a sign reading "Welcome to Calgary, Eddie the Eagle." Unfortunately, this also led to his other nickname. You see, Edwards was extremely far-sighted, and thus had to wear thick glasses at all times. When he arrived at the Calgary airport it was 2:30 a.m., and the automatic doors were turned off. Striding towards his welcoming sign, with skis resting on his shoulder, Michael walked right into the glass doors, and was dubbed "Mr. Magoo" for the duration of the Games. Despite this bumpy start, Michael Edwards became an instant fan favourite—perhaps proving the old adage that everyone loves an underdog.

Edwards's eyesight problems definitely hampered his competitiveness. In order to see, he had to wear his glasses underneath his ski mask. But the glasses steamed up, making vision nearly impossible, and he finished dead last in both the 70-metre and 90-metre jumps. Nevertheless, the crowds admired his grit and perseverance. At the closing ceremonies, Frank King, the president of the Olympic Organizing Committee, paid tribute to Edwards, noting that "some competitors have won gold, some have broken records, and some of you have even soared like an eagle." It was the first and so far the only time that an individual athlete has been acknowledged in a closing speech. The crowd went wild, and 60,000 voices in unison chanted "Eddie! Eddie!"

Unfortunately, the International Olympic Committee took a dim view of Edwards and his participation, and two years later instituted what has come to be known as the "Eddie the Eagle Rule." The new rules stated that Olympic competitors could rank no lower than 50th in the world in their sport. As a result, Edwards failed to qualify for both the 1992 and the 1994 Olympic Games.

Michael Edwards has never lost his enthusiasm for the Olympics, though, and in 2010 he was selected as one of the torchbearers for the Vancouver Winter Games. And his story just might make it onto the silver screen one of these days. As he also told Stuart Jeffries in his 2007 interview, negotiations were underway for the film rights to the "Eddie the Eagle" story. Michael felt that Tom Cruise or Brad Pitt would be great choices to play him in the movie.

THE LIFE AND TIMES
OF THE STANLEY CUP

What the World Series is to Americans, the Stanley Cup is to Canadians—and has been for more than a century. The origins of the Stanley Cup date back to 1892. Since then, over 2,000 individuals have lived their dreams and hoisted the coveted Cup. To reach that pinnacle today, teams play 82 regular season games and up to 28 playoff games. Each individual from a winning team is allotted a single day with the Cup of his dreams. But with the mug's history of abuse and neglect, a number of those dreams seem not to have gone quite as planned!

For example, losing the Stanley Cup has been quite a common occurrence over the years. After the Ottawa Silver Seven won it all in 1905, the players decided to take Stanley for a night on the town. After indulging in a few spirits, one celebrant boasted of his punting skills and claimed he could kick it across the Rideau Canal. Not realizing the self-proclaimed placekicker had actually booted the Cup right *into* the Canal, the team continued on partying. Fortunately the Cup was recovered. In 1907, after the Montreal Canadiens had a team picture taken with the Cup, they forgot it in the photographer's studio for several months. When they finally came back for it (after it was reported stolen), they found that the photographer's mother was using it as a vase for her geraniums. In 2009 Sidney Crosby made sure he wasn't going to lose the Cup: he slept with it.

The Cup has also undergone its fair share of abuse. Learning the tough way that the Cup does not double as a life jacket, Pittsburgh Penguin Phil Bourque's victory lap around Mario Lemieux's pool ended just as you might have expected—with the Cup at the bottom of the deep end for the night. Apparently, Patrick Roy didn't get the memo from Bourque, because two years later the Cup mysteriously ended up amongst his snorkel gear at the bottom of his pool. Nick Kypreos and Brian Noonan seem to have played out their childhood dreams with the Cup. Kypreos allegedly had a heated game of kick-the-can with it, while Noonan supposedly used the Cup as a rolling pin to do some baking. After one of his six championships, Mark Messier reportedly dented the Cup pretty badly and had to take it to his mechanic to be fixed.

Since the top of Lord Stanley's trophy is a cup or large bowl, it seems only logical that one might choose to eat and drink out of it and, indeed, many have enjoyed champagne from it. But perhaps nobody did use it for consumptive purposes quite like Doug Weight from the Carolina Hurricanes.

He celebrated by filling the Cup with gallons of ice cream, M&Ms, chocolate sauce and marshmallows, making the world's most prestigious ice cream sundae. In 1980, Clark Gillies' dog got a chance to gobble down some kibbles out of the Cup.

Perhaps Sylvain Lefebvre gave the Stanley Cup its most serious (even reverent) role, when his baby was baptized in it. And on the other end of the spectrum, the Cup played perhaps one of its least dignified roles in 2008. A week after winning the Cup, Detroit's Kris Draper found himself pulling out the disinfectant and paper towels when his newborn daughter answered a call of nature while she was sitting in the Cup.

Of all the players who had their day with the Stanley Cup, perhaps Phil Bourque left the biggest mark on it—literally. In 1991 during his time with the mug, he dismantled it while attempting to fix a rattling noise. While he was doing so, he decided to etch his name on the inside of one of the silver rings, writing "Enjoy it, Phil Bubba Bourque, '91 Penguins."

You know the old saying: if only the walls could talk. Well, if only the Stanley Cup could talk... On second thought, perhaps it's better that the mug keeps quiet. Some things should be left in the vault.

3

HISTORY IN THE MAKING

OH CANADA!

Thousands of kilometres of travelling had been logged and 420 minutes of play were in the books. On Thursday, September 28, 1972, millions of Canadians were in front of their televisions, tuned in to the final game of the most emotion-filled series in hockey history: the first ever Canada-Russia series. That day, a team of hard-nosed Canadians, but without stars Bobby Orr and Bobby Hull, took to the ice at the Luzhniki Ice Palace in Moscow for the eighth and final game against Russia.

The tension had been building, not just throughout the series, but for years. It is hard for anyone born after the fall of the Berlin Wall in 1989 to comprehend the extent to which the Cold War dominated the collective consciousness of both East and West. In all aspects of daily life, it was "us" versus "them." And, complicating that East-West rivalry, there was a long-simmering Canadian resentment that had finally bubbled over. You see, Canadians had/have long believed that they have the best hockey players in the world. However, for decades, Canada's National Hockey League players, who were professionals because they received a salary, had been barred from competing against amateurs. The problem was that the Russian players, while defined as "amateurs," were state-supported under the communist system, and therefore were pros in all but name. As a result, the Soviets dominated international hockey tournaments, not to mention the Olympics, because they competed against younger, truly amateur Canadian teams. The Canadian public, incensed, demanded that the playing field be levelled.

And that was what the Canada-Russia series was all about. At long last, it was to feature "our" best against "their" best. Canadians smugly congratulated themselves that their NHL players would clean the ice with the Russians. It would be a wipe-out.

Or maybe not. The first game, on September 2, 1972, was played in the Montreal Forum, home of the legendary Montreal Canadiens, the very heart and soul of hockey in Canada! Canadians were barely able to contain their excitement. We would have vindication at last! And then, the unthinkable happened: the Russians not only defeated the Canadians, they humiliated them, taking the first game 7-3. The nation went into collective shock. After three more games in Canada, the Russians led the series with two wins, one loss, and one tie.

The series resumed in Moscow two weeks later, and the Canadian team lost the first game. The future looked bleak, as the Canadians would have to win all three remaining games to take the series. Conventional wisdom said that it couldn't be done. But then, the tide seemed to turn. The Canadians won the next two games, but could they maintain the momentum? It all came down to one game. Three periods. Sixty minutes.

At last, September 28, 1972, arrived. It was Game 8. The referee made his way to centre ice, dropped the puck, and the game began. The pace was torrid, the physicality intense, and emotions were high. The Soviets opened the scoring. Less than three minutes later, frustrated by a series of questionable penalty calls, Canadian Jean-Paul Parisé looked poised to "lumber-jack" West German referee Josef Kompalla with his stick, and received a penalty and a game misconduct. Nevertheless, the dogged Canadians replied with a tally by Phil Esposito, which refocused the group. The slick Soviets added another goal from Vladimir Lutchenko, the Canadians added one from Brad Park, and the first period closed knotted at 2-2.

The second period started much the same way with the finesse of the Soviets potting them another lead on a goal by Vladimir Shadrin, but again the tenacious Canadians replied when Bill White slipped one by Soviet Union goaltender Vladislav Tretiak. But, the stalemate was broken again with two consecutive Soviet goals. The second period ended with a 5-3 Soviet lead.

Because the Soviets had scored more goals during the previous seven games, they needed only a tie to win the series—the pressure was on the Canadians, who had to win. The third period began with Esposito notching his second of the game, cutting the lead to 5-4. Canada poured on the pressure, but the Soviets turned aside wave after wave of Canadian assaults until, with under 10 minutes to go, Yvan Cournoyer potted a rebound past Tretiak to tie the game. The Canadians redoubled their efforts and kept the Soviets bottled in. But the winning goal was elusive as again the Soviets managed to withstand the barrage of tempered rubber from the Canucks. The clock ticked into the final minute. Peter Mahovlich changed for Paul Henderson on the fly and Henderson made his way to the Russian zone. Under 40 seconds remained when Esposito took a weak shot and Tretiak steered it aside ... right to the stick of Henderson, who was waiting in front of the Soviet net. With the clock at 34 seconds, Henderson snuck one by the unflappable Tretiak to give Canada a 6-5 lead. The Canadian team stormed the ice, and the 3,000 Canadian fans in attendance erupted, joined by millions back home who exploded into raucous cheers. The Soviets couldn't believe they'd let it all slip away, and were still in shock as Canada held on for the final 34 seconds to take the series.

To this day, most Canadians alive at the time can still remember where they were when Henderson scored that glorious goal, and in their mind's eye can still see that iconic image of him, his arms raised in jubilation. It has become part of Canada's folklore. Oh Canada!

HAMMERIN' HANK

Many professional athletes call attention to themselves with flashy play and on-field antics—superstars such as hockey's Alexander Ovechkin and football's Terrell Owens immediately come to mind. Indeed, few players can manage to fly "under the radar" and still maintain name recognition for themselves. In baseball, much of the spotlight has been reserved for the Yankees in New York and the Red Sox in Boston; being a member of the Milwaukee Brewers and Atlanta Braves didn't exactly lend itself to the same stardom as an association with the big-market teams. However, that's exactly how humble Hank Aaron liked it.

"Hammerin' Hank" was a low-key player whose calling card was steadiness rather than showmanship. He was inconspicuous off the field and businesslike on it. He carried himself well and didn't walk with the swagger or panache of players like Barry Bonds. Nevertheless, slowly but steadily, Hank Aaron stalked the ghost of the "Great Bambino."

FAST FACT

Barry Bonds eventually surpassed **Hank Aaron**'s record, and is now the all-time home-run hitter, with a total of 762. However, Bonds's record has been tainted by ongoing allegations that he used illegal steroids. Thus, to many, "Hammerin' Hank" remains the true home-run king.

At the end of the 1973 season, the unassuming Aaron had 713 home runs, just one shy of Babe Ruth's record—a record that most observers thought would never be broken. As he came ever closer to Ruth's total, Aaron received an onslaught of fan mail and letters of encouragement, but he also received hate mail and death threats to such an extent that the Atlanta Police Department assigned him a bodyguard. A lot of the hate mail was racial in nature, as white supremacists couldn't handle the idea that Aaron, a Black man, could possibly surpass the record held by Babe Ruth, who was White.

But, in his usual fashion, Aaron responded to the naysayers and bigots not by words, but by actions. On opening day in 1974, Aaron jacked a dinger in Cincinnati to tie Ruth's record, putting the Braves' slugger one home run away from baseball immortality. The next game, in an attempt to allow him to hit the record-breaking home run at home in Atlanta, Braves manager Eddie Mathews benched Aaron, using three pinch-hitters. This, however, did not sit well with commissioner Bowie Kuhn, who ordered the Braves to play Aaron in the last game of the three-game series or face serious penalties. Aaron did play but fell short of the record, with two strikeouts and a groundout.

But the next night, on Monday April 8, 1974, in front of 53,273 spectators, Hank Aaron changed baseball history forever. It was the fourth inning, with a runner at first, and Dodgers pitcher Al Downing waiting for Aaron to step up to the dish. Aaron set his stance and took the first pitch low and inside for a ball. But on the second pitch, Aaron made sure that the high fastball would not reach the catcher. He tattooed the ball deep towards left centerfield, clearing the wall and landing in the Dodgers' bullpen in the glove of relief pitcher Tom House. History was made! "Hammerin' Hank" Aaron rounded the bases to the deafening applause of the Braves' faithful. When asked to comment after the game, Aaron stated, with his typical modesty, "I'm thankful to God it's all over."

WILT, THE ONE-MAN SHOW

In the world of sports, every so often something happens that nobody thought possible. One of these times was on the evening of March 2, 1962. The sport was basketball, the player Wilt Chamberlain, and the final score was Philadelphia Warriors 169, New York Knicks 147. A high score by basketball standards, or virtually any sports standards for that matter, but the team score is not the anomaly here. Of the 169 points scored by Philadelphia, Wilt "the Stilt" Chamberlain was personally responsible for 100 of them! The Stilt had 63 shot attempts from the field—36 of which he drained—and also made 28 of a possible 32 free throws, which together made up his 100-point night. Consider this: A basketball game is only 48 minutes long. That means Chamberlain was attempting a shot once every 45.7 seconds from the field. In his amazing performance he scored 23 points in the first quarter, 18 in the second, 28 in the third, and 31 in the fourth.

Of course, the 100 points amassed by Chamberlain is a record, but he also set a few others that March evening. The

63 attempted shots as well as the 36 made are both NBA records, and his 28 free throws tied the NBA record.

The Knicks, not wanting to become a part of history that evening, began fouling everyone except Chamberlain so that his teammates would have to shoot, thus keeping the ball out of the Stilt's hands. Some of the Knicks players became very upset with the Warriors because every ball was being passed to Chamberlain, sometimes when open lay-ups were available. But the Warriors stuck with this tried-and-true strategy: "if it ain't broke don't fix it." They kept passing, and Chamberlain kept sinking shot after shot.

As the game wound into its final minute, Chamberlain was two points shy of the 100 mark. Then, with only 46 seconds left, he sank his final basket of the game. The 100-point record was set!

Unfortunately, there had been no television coverage that night. Thus, after a full-court rush from the excited crowd had subsided, and the game was officially in the history books, nothing remained of it but the box score, the taped radio broadcast, and some memories. Unbelievably, the performance of a lifetime—and perhaps the performance of all time—had been witnessed by a mere 4,000 or so lucky fans watching live NBA basketball in Hershey, Pennsylvania, that March evening nearly half a century ago.

"HOWE" FITTING

There are moments in sports that seem somehow pre-ordained. The timing is just too perfect, the moment is larger than life, a series of events plays out flawlessly. On the evening of October 15, 1989, one of those special moments took place. On that surreal night, it seemed as if the gods of hockey themselves intervened. They descended upon the Edmonton Coliseum, and Wayne Gretzky was their chosen instrument.

To that point, Gretzky had played the majority of his NHL career with the Edmonton Oilers, where he had amassed 1,669 points before being traded to the Los Angeles Kings prior to the 1988–89 season. With the Kings, he had tacked on another 180 points, putting his career point total at 1,849—just one shy of Gordie Howe's all-time record. Like a dog that makes its way home after being lost, Gretzky had found his way back to Edmonton—his true hockey home—on that historic October evening. The Edmonton fans still loved Gretzky as their own, and rightfully so. The Canadian-bred phenomenon had led the Oilers to four Stanley Cup championships during the 1980s. It was fitting, therefore, that when the 1989–90 season schedule was drawn up, the hockey gods ordained that Wayne would come home, to be given his chance for hockey immortality in the Edmonton Coliseum.

Gretzky quickly tied Howe's record only 4:32 into the game with an assist on a Bernie Nicholls goal, sending the fans into a frenzy. Gretzky now had the entire game to get one more point, and the crowd nearly exploded every time he touched the puck. But the hockey gods, being whimsical, kept Gretzky at bay as the game wore on. The Kings and Oilers were locked in an exciting see-saw affair that saw Gretzky's Kings down 4-3 in the third period. The suspense was overwhelming; it seemed as though every person in the arena was holding his or her breath. The gods were in control of the moment.

When the clock hit the last minute in the third period, The Great One already had been on the ice for three minutes. Seeing their hero tire, when he was so close to making history, the Edmonton crowd began chanting "Gretzky, Gretzky, Gretzky" to urge him on. Then the Kings rushed up the ice. As they gained the offensive zone, Gretzky broke toward the net and picked up a bouncing puck. He corralled it near the left post, stick-handled to his backhand, and sent it floating past Edmonton goalie Bill Ranford.

At that moment, Gretzky went from being The Great One to being the greatest of all time, with point number 1,851. The gods released their hold on the fans and deafening cheers broke out, growing to a three-minute standing ovation. Players from both teams swarmed Gretzky, congratulating him. The city of Edmonton appreciated Gretzky so much that the game was stopped for a special presentation, during which the Oilers and the National Hockey League praised him for what he meant to hockey, in the city and in the league.

After a 15-minute interruption, the game continued and regulation play ended in a 4-4 tie. Not quite done yet, and wanting to put an exclamation point on the moment, the hockey gods went to work for one final act. At 3:24 of overtime, Gretzky rolled out from behind the net—his "office"—and put another backhand behind Ranford to win the game. Again, the crowd roared, cheering despite the home team's loss.

That night in Edmonton, it seemed as though there were supernatural forces in play. And perhaps Wayne Gretzky was one of them: a living, breathing hockey god.

GIBSON'S FINEST

Athletes often play when injured, fuelled by self-discipline and motivated by devotion to their team. Frequently, however, they end up doing more harm than good. Too many times, banged-up, aging greats refuse to give up their spot in the line-up when it would have been better to let someone healthier step in. But there are rare occasions when we see a truly gutsy performance from an injured warrior that reminds us of what sport is and how great it can be. Sometimes, as an athlete—no matter how lousy you feel or how badly you have been playing—you get that sense that there isn't anything you can't do. When this happens, all the pains and doubts of injury evaporate, if only fleetingly. There is one such moment in professional sport that epitomizes this phenomenon.

Baseball's Los Angeles Dodgers were in tough against the favoured Oakland Athletics in the 1988 World Series. Making a dire situation worse, Dodgers team leader and veteran Kirk Gibson had a pulled left hamstring and a sprained medial collateral ligament in his right knee from the previous series against the New York Mets, in which he had sparked the Dodgers with two game-winning home runs. With Gibson out of the lineup, the Dodgers looked as though they couldn't match the power of the Athletics bench, which was bolstered by the home-run tandem of Mark McGwire and José Canseco. It seemed as though the Dodgers were David to the Athletics' Goliath.

Gibson could barely walk, let alone play baseball at his accustomed level. In fact, Gibson spent the first 8½ innings of the World Series stuck in the trainer's room, tending to his injuries. Several ice packs and cortisone injections later, Gibson still sat in the trainer's room, watching the game on TV, when he heard a comment he didn't like coming from one of the game announcers. While on the air, NBC's Vin Scully noted that Gibson wasn't even on the bench so he was definitely out for any pinch-hitting or ninth-inning heroics. The half-dressed Gibson took exception to the remarks and began putting on his uniform. While he suited up, Gibson got clubhouse attendant Mitch Poole to set up a batting tee and to fetch manager Tommy Lasorda.

Lasorda, confused, made his way to see Gibson, wondering what was up. When the manager got there, to his surprise he saw a still-hobbling Gibson. Gibson told Lasorda to pinch-hit him in the ninth spot for the pitcher. Lasorda told him to wait in the clubhouse for the time being, so Oakland wouldn't see Gibson on the bench and know their plan.

Back in the dugout, Lasorda was watching the bottom of the ninth with his Dodgers trailing 4-3. Oakland's future Hall of Fame closer Dennis Eckersley was on the mound and throwing Aspirins as he retired the first two batters in the ninth. That left one out and the eighth spot pinch-hitter, Mike Davis, at the dish with another pinch-hitter in Dave Anderson at the on-deck circle. Davis worked a walk, setting the stage for Gibson. Lasorda pulled Anderson from the on-deck circle and the crowd waited in suspense to see who was going to pinch hit.

Gibson emerged from the dugout and struggled up the top steps on to the field, while an ecstatic Los Angeles crowd cheered on their wounded hero. Gibson hobbled all the way to the batter's box in front of the equally astonished Dodgers and Athletics. Gibson, who hadn't swung a bat in three days, was standing on legs about as useful as wooden pegs, facing the game's best closing pitcher. Things still didn't look good, but the Dodger Nation had its fingers crossed.

Gibson sat steady in the box, but soon found himself with a count of 2-2 after two painful hacks at fastballs he was nowhere near. Gibson looked overmatched but managed to watch a fifth pitch go by. With two outs and a full count in the bottom of the ninth, and himself representing the winning run, Gibson remembered what Dodgers scout Mel Didier said: look for Eckersley to throw a back door slider on 3-2.

Eckersley did just that and Gibson was waiting for it. He stepped into his swing and connected flush with the pitch, sending the ball soaring. On contact, the entire stadium knew it was gone and erupted with deafening cheers as the ball was in flight toward the right-field bleachers.

Gibson, with a wobbly and painful-looking stride, rounded the bases—the hero once again. The excited Gibson pumped his fist forcefully as he passed second base, and his face showed no sign of pain as he basked in his game-winning round-tripper. On the final leg of the trot he "high-fived" the third base coach and came home into the jubilant arms of his teammates. The Dodgers took the game 5-3.

Despite the injuries and the odds, Kirk Gibson came through with one of the grittiest performances in sports history. Gibson's only at-bat of the entire series inspired his teammates, who went on to win the best-of-seven series in five games.

You can't make up a story like this.

150-METRE CLASH

The men's 100-metre dash is the shortest outdoor sprint race in competitive athletics, and the winner of the race at the Summer Olympic Games generally claims the unofficial title of "world's fastest man." On July 27, 1996, Canada's Donovan Bailey took home the gold medal—and the title—for his victory at the XXVI Olympic Games in Atlanta. Not only did Bailey win the 100-metre dash, but he did so in record time: 9.84 seconds.

In Canada, Bailey's victory was particularly meaningful, since it helped wipe away the national shame that Canadians had felt for the previous eight years. At the 1988 Seoul Olympics, Canadian Ben Johnson had set a new world record in the 100-metre dash, only to be disqualified three days later after failing a drug test. With Bailey's gold medal, national pride was redeemed. Or was it?

American sprinter Michael Johnson (no relation to Ben) had also taken a gold medal at the Atlanta Games—he ran the

200-metre race at a record speed of 19.32 seconds. So what, you ask? Well, if you divide Johnson's time of 19.32 seconds in half, the result is an average of 9.66 seconds per 100 metres. Thus, it could be claimed that Johnson was actually the "world's fastest man"—which is precisely what some sports commentators, including NBC's Bob Costas, began to do.

In the ensuing debate, it was pointed out that a 200-metre race usually results in a faster "per metre" average time, since runners have extra distance to compensate for the slower starting time—an advantage not available to 100-metre racers. In fact, when Johnson won the 200-metre race at the Atlanta Games, he had run the first 100 metres in 10.12 seconds—more than a quarter of a second slower than Bailey's time in the 100-metre. This was pretty arcane stuff, though, and didn't really resolve the issue of which man was faster.

In early 1997, Johnson upped the ante, and began doing promotional ads on television, where he referred to himself as "the world's fastest man." Bailey at first refused to be drawn into the controversy, stating that as far as he was concerned, his triumph at the 100-metre race in Atlanta meant the title was his. The dispute continued both on and off the air, however, and it was eventually decided that staging another, "made for TV," race would be the only way to resolve the issue.

The next thing to be decided was the length of the race itself. Bailey's specialty was the 100-metre dash, while Johnson dominated the field for the 200-metre event. After discussion between the two camps, it was decided that they would split the difference, and the race would be 150 metres. The winner would take home a prize purse of $1.5 million, while the loser would receive $500,000—surely enough to remove the sting of the defeat. Toronto's SkyDome was selected as the site of the race, giving "home town" advantage to Bailey.

On May 31, 1997, sports fans—both Canadian and American—began streaming into the SkyDome. The atmosphere in the stadium was electric. It was north versus south, Canada versus the United States—an intercontinental battle. The course would be 75 metres of curved track, and 75 metres of straight track.

The two racers took the starting blocks, with Bailey on the inside lane and Johnson on the outside lane. BANG! Before the echo of the starting gun had faded, the two men were blistering down the track. By mid-race, Bailey had a commanding lead. At the 110-metre mark, as Bailey dug in for the final 40 metres, Johnson pulled back, grabbing his leg. Bailey looked back and, supremely confident at this point, waved for Johnson to "come on." But Johnson was finished, apparently having injured his left quadriceps muscle.

Bailey crossed the finish line at 14.99 seconds—much slower than his Olympic time. However, a win is a win, and he grabbed the Canadian flag and did a victory lap around the track. He was now, officially, the world's fastest man! In a post-race interview, Bailey, who was obviously angry with Johnson, added insult to injury by stating: "He didn't pull up. He's just a chicken. I think we should run this race again so I could whip his ass one more time." Johnson's reaction hasn't been recorded.

Yet another race might have occurred, but both men were plagued by injuries following the race. Johnson would not compete for the rest of the year because of his quadriceps injury. Later in 1997, Bailey broke a bone in his foot, and before the end of the year he tore his Achilles tendon—a severe injury from which he never fully recovered.

Eventually, the point would become moot. Bailey's Olympic record of 9.84 seconds in the 100-metre race would last until 2008, when it was broken at the Beijing Olympics, by

FAST FACT

Usain Bolt was participating in the Beijing Olympics when his birthday rolled around on August 21, 2008. He had just won two gold medals (see *"The Olympic Lightning Bolt,"* p. 113), and was poised to win his third, when he received a unique birthday gift. It was a shoe, but it wasn't just any shoe. In fact, it was a gold-medal shoe, if there can be said to be such a thing. The donor was Tommie Smith, who had won the 200-metre race at the 1968 Mexico City Olympics. Smith's remarkable Olympic story is told elsewhere in this book (see *"Podium Protest,"* p. 146). We do not know if the "Lightning Bolt" has had the shoe gilded or not.

a run of 9.69 seconds. Johnson's 200-metre Olympic record of 19.32 seconds was broken in 2009, with a new record time of 19.19 seconds.

It was a runner from Jamaica who broke both records. As of January 2011, the disputed title belongs to neither Donovan Bailey nor Michael Johnson. Rather, the honour is now held by Usain Bolt: the world's fastest man.

4

A MOMENT OF SILENCE

THE
THUNDERING HERD

It was November 14, 1970, and the Thundering Herd, the Marshall University football team from Huntington, West Virginia, had just lost 17-14 to East Carolina University at Ficklen Stadium, in Greenville, North Carolina. With only one game remaining in their season, against Ohio University, the Herd boarded an airplane for home and a week of practice and recuperation. It was the only time that year the team had taken a flight.

At 6:38 p.m., Southern Airways Flight 932, departing from Kinston, NC, and destined for Huntington, lifted off for its projected 52-minute flight. The flight was chartered for the Herd's 37 players, the five-member coaching staff, three team administrators, 25 fans, and five crew. The flight aboard the 95-seat DC-9 was routine, and at 7:23 p.m., the pilot radioed Tri-State Airport serving Huntington, announcing the flight's descent to 5,000 feet in preparation for landing. With a mixture of rain and fog, landing conditions were not ideal, but it wasn't anything that the pilots hadn't handled before. Then, approaching from the west at 7:34 p.m., the flight's crew reported that they were passing the airport's outer markers and ready to land. The tower cleared their approach and the crew commenced the final descent. At 7:36 p.m., disaster struck. Flight 932 was off course.

Onlookers from the nearby Ashland oil refinery thought everything was normal, other than that the descending plane was approaching lower than usual. Then the control tower and refinery workers saw a red glow in the distance. Some 1,689 metres (5541 feet) to the west of the runway, the aircraft had struck a tree. The impact forced the plane deeper into the surrounding bush, carving out a swath 29 metres (95 feet) wide and 85 metres (279 feet) long. As it cut down trees, the aircraft began losing pieces of its nose and its right wing, causing it to plunge to the right and crash nose-first into a hollow. At 1,286 metres (4219 feet) short of the runway and a mere 69 metres (226 feet) south of the middle marker, the plane finally came to rest, and then exploded into flames. There were no survivors, and the exact cause of the disaster was never determined.

Faced with this unparalleled catastrophe, university administrators considered permanently shutting down the football program. However, new head coach Jack Lengyel, the four surviving players (who had not been aboard Flight 932 that fateful night), and members of the community all insisted that the Herd contest the 1971 season, as a tribute to the fallen athletes.

The Thundering Herd had a record of two wins and eight losses in the 1971 season, and throughout the 1970s lost more football games than any other college program in the United States. However, football survived and rebuilt in Huntington, and in 1984, the Herd posted their first winning record in two decades. This was followed in succeeding years by eight conference titles, five straight bowl wins, and two national championships. Thus, despite the devastating events of November 14, 1970, the spirit of sports eventually triumphed in Huntington, rising from the ashes of a heartbreaking tragedy.

On December 12, 2006, *We Are Marshall*, a film examining the tragedy and its aftermath, premiered in Huntington, West Virginia.

DISASTER
AT LE MANS

Since 1923, France has been home to one of the racing world's première events—the 24 Hours of Le Mans, also known as the "Grand Prix of Endurance." Held every June, the race is driven over 8.38 miles (13.5 km) on a combination of racetrack and closed public roads. The winning car is the one that covers the most ground over the gruelling 24-hour period.

When the race first debuted, participating cars could rarely exceed 60 mph (97 km/h), seatbelts were unknown, and little, if any, thought had been given to the safety of spectators. For decades, there were no rules governing either the number of drivers assigned to each car, or the length of time each driver could be behind the wheel. This would change, but not before the most catastrophic accident in motorsports history.

Before the 1955 race began, Mercedes driver Pierre Levegh had expressed concern about the dangerously high speed of the cars in the narrow "pit straight." Cars now reached top speeds in excess of 190 mph (310 km/h), and Levegh believed that a signal system had to be devised so drivers knew when a participant was making a pit stop. Levegh hoped this would help prevent abrupt breaking and high-speed crashes. His suggestions were ignored, and the race went on as scheduled.

On June 11, 1955, some 300,000 spectators were on hand, and the Le Mans marathon had just entered its third hour. Jaguar driver Mike Hawthorn, who was leading the pack, got the signal from his crew to pull into the pits and refuel. Hawthorn hit the brakes and made a sharp right turn to reach his crew. Austin-Healey driver Lance Macklin, following close behind, had no choice but to swerve left to avoid a collision. Behind Macklin was Pierre Levegh. Unable to swerve or stop in time, Levegh barrelled into the low, sloping rear end of the Austin-Healey at 150 mph (240 km/h). Had it been another car, Levegh might have simply run into its rear, but the sloping shape of the Austin-Healey, in effect, acted as a launch pad, causing Levegh's Mercedes to hurdle end over end into the crowd.

Levegh was thrown out of the somersaulting car; his skull was crushed upon impact and he died instantly. Car parts began to fly in every direction. The hood, like a flying guillotine, decapitated several people in the crowd's tightly crammed front row. Then, the chassis, engine, and front axle broke loose and hurtled into the spectators, causing multiple fatalities. Next, the fuel tank exploded, turning what was left of the car into an inferno.

The body of the Mercedes contained a high percentage of magnesium, an element which has a very low flashpoint. This, coupled with the high velocity of the flying chassis, increased the intensity of the flaming debris, sending white-hot embers onto the track and into the crowd. To make matters worse, rescue workers didn't realize that water only strengthened magnesium-based fires. When they attempted to put out the burning Mercedes, they instead created a fiery death trap that lasted for several hours. It was a scene of unmitigated horror, and hospitals for miles around over-flowed with the injured and the dying. Ultimately, more than 80 men, women, and children died that day, and more than a hundred others were injured, many critically.

The event organizers realized that if they stopped the race, the outbound traffic would prevent the ambulances which were converging on the scene from getting through. Thus, reluctantly, they decided to allow the race to continue. The rest of the Mercedes team withdrew, but the Jaguar teamed declined to do so. Ironically, it was Mike Hawthorn, the Jaguar driver whose sudden pit stop had begun the chain of events leading to the accident, who would go on to win. He would die in a motor accident four years later, at the age of 29.

As is so often the case following a disaster of this mag-nitude, racing officials and drivers alike were forced to con-sider new safety measures. Racing teams in future would be composed of three drivers, with limits on the amount of time any one individual could be in the driver's seat. John Fitch, who had been Pierre Levegh's co-driver, went on to become a major safety advocate and would be actively involved in developing safer cars and racetracks for decades to come. He would found a company named Impact Attenuation Inc. At Le Mans itself, shortly after the tragedy the Grandstand and the pit area were torn down and rebuilt, with enhanced safety features for both spectators and crew. But nothing could ever bring back those who had died in Le Mans that tragic day in June 1955.

URUGUAYAN AIR FORCE FLIGHT 571

On October 13, 1972, Uruguayan Air Force Flight 571 departed from Montevideo, Uruguay, en route to Santiago, Chile. On board were 40 passengers—players and affiliates of Stella Maris College's "Old Christians" Rugby Union team—and five crew members. The flight was routine, and the pilot notified air traffic control that he was over central Chile, preparing for his descent into Santiago. But the pilot had failed to account for the strong head wind, and the descent into Santiago airport was initiated far too soon. Falling below the cloud ceiling, the airplane emerged in the midst of the Andes, on a collision course with a looming mountain peak.

The first impact completely dislodged the right wing. The plane ricocheted off the first peak and struck another, this time severing the left wing. The fuselage—the central body of the aircraft to which the wings and tail are attached— hurtled onwards. After careening down the mountain, what was left of the plane finally came to rest in a snow bank, somewhere in the uncharted alpine wilderness between Chile and Argentina.

Miraculously, only twelve people died in the crash itself, although five of the more seriously injured victims were dead by the next morning, followed by a sixth a few days later. A week after the crash, 27 battered rugby players remained alive. The only doctor on the flight had died during the crash, leaving medical care to two of the players who were medical students. They did their best to tend to their injured comrades, making improvised splints and braces from the wreckage of the plane, but more of the passengers would succumb to their injuries in the weeks to come.

At first, the survivors decided it was best to wait for rescue. But after 11 days atop the frigid mountain, they received grim news over a small transistor radio: the search for the plane had been called off.

Survival at high altitudes in the middle of winter requires a very high caloric intake. However, since Flight 571 would normally have been only a few hours in duration, provisions aboard the plane were limited to a few chocolate bars, nougat, some crackers and jam, and several bottles of wine. Although strictly rationed, the food would not last for long, and the survivors were faced with a horrific choice: either they must choose death, by starvation and hypothermia, or they must force themselves to consume the bodies of the deceased, many of whom had been their classmates and friends. It was the most difficult decision any of them would ever confront. Eventually, they retrieved the bodies; using a piece of broken glass, they began cutting off pieces of frozen flesh.

On October 29, further catastrophe struck. An avalanche cascaded down the mountain and buried eight of the survivors who had been sleeping. Those who were not trapped tried to rescue their friends, digging with bare hands, but to no avail: 19 survivors now remained. Three of these would die in the weeks to come.

It was now apparent that their only hope for survival lay in escaping from the mountainside. However, this in itself was a daunting task: all of the survivors were by now malnourished, many were injured, all lacked proper winter clothing, the alpine terrain was treacherous and exhausting to navigate, and snow blindness was a constant hazard. Nonetheless, on December 12, Roberto Canessa, Fernando Parrado, and Antonio Vizitín set off from the crash site to seek help, taking with them a three-man sleeping bag fashioned from materials and insulation salvaged from the plane. On the third day of their trek they reached the top of the mountain. To their dismay, a seemingly endless sea of mountain peaks stretched out before them. However, Parrado spotted a small trail along a valley in the distance that he gauged to be a road. With the hike taking longer and expending more energy than anticipated, and rations running short, it was decided that Vizitín would return to the fuselage.

After several more days of hiking, Canessa and Parrado reached a narrow valley and began to follow the river that weaved through it. Seeing scattered signs of human occupation they continued, and after nine days spotted three men on horseback on the other side of the river, their first contact with the outside world in over two months.

Back at the crash site, the remaining survivors heard on the radio that Parrado and Canessa had been successful. For the first time in months, there was real hope of rescue. On December 22, two helicopters arrived, carrying search and rescue climbers, and guided by Parrado. Only half of the survivors could be airlifted out that day, but the next morning, at 10:00 o'clock, the remaining eight survivors were taken to safety.

After 72 days in the remote Andean wilderness, 16 young men managed to survive, despite appalling conditions and horrendous choices. Known in Latin America as *El Milagro de los Andes* (the Miracle of the Andes), the ill-fated Flight 571 remains one of the worst sports-related disasters in history. Nevertheless, it is also a testament to the courage and resilience of the human spirit.

UNITED
WE STAND

In times of peace and prosperity, we tend to underestimate the significance of sport in society, often seeing sporting events as simply providing an opportunity to relax and unwind after the events of the day. Times of crisis, however, offer us a chance to witness the true potential of sport to be more than mere entertainment, serving instead as a unifying and healing force in a community.

When the World Trade Center towers were struck on September 11, 2001, the United States, and much of the world, went into a state of collective shock. However, in the midst of tragedy and chaos, it was baseball—that most American of sports—around which the citizens of New York rallied. With the New York Yankees making a run at the World Series that year, Yankee Stadium became a place of solace for the people of New York—a venue for collective mourning and an outlet for the pain and grief that followed the 9/11 attacks.

Following the destruction of the twin towers, it would have been understandable had New Yorkers been reluctant to gather together in large groups, lest they present a target for further attacks. Indeed, there was some discussion about the suitability of continuing with the baseball season, because of the potential danger involved, but also because it might have been interpreted as disrespectful to the victims. However, although delayed, the World Series was held. And then, a remarkable thing happened. Perhaps because of the continuity that sports represented in a dangerous and changing world, or perhaps simply as a means of demonstrating solidarity with their fellow citizens, New Yorkers turned out in tremendous numbers for the playoffs. As New York mayor Rudy Giuliani said of the sell-out crowd of over 56,000 at Yankee Stadium in the first round of playoffs: "[It was] important for the spirit of the city. ... The fact that all of these people showed up unafraid, undeterred, I think it's absolutely terrific." When President George W. Bush made a personal appearance in New York at Game 3 of the World Series, disregarding safety concerns by throwing out the first pitch, Giuliani echoed the sentiments of many New Yorkers when he stated: "[This] shows we're not afraid, we're undeterred and that life is moving on the way it should."

In the aftermath of 9/11, games were altered to include reminders of the recent events by holding commemorative ceremonies, singing patriotic songs between innings, and remembering past moments of triumph and success. *USA Today* writer Erik Brady stated this phenomenon most succinctly: "Ballparks became home to sacramental ceremony. It seemed natural to salute and sing and cry and then settle in for a game that meant exactly nothing and everything all at once." Robert S. Brown, a professor of Communications at Ashland University, noted in his study on sports and healing in America that "sport often addresses the nation's pain, inviting spectators to deal with their feelings from a number of perspectives." Baseball therefore became an important part of the healing process for the entire nation.

On April 16, 2006, a horrific tragedy occurred at Virginia Polytechnic Institute and State University (Virginia Tech), in Blacksburg, Virgina. A South Korean exchange student, Seung-Hui Cho, in two separate attacks, killed 33 staff and students and left 17 others injured before turning the gun on himself. The massacre was the largest peacetime shooting incident by a single gunman in United States history. The following spring, at a commemorative Convocation ceremony, poet and professor Nikki Giovanni paid tribute to the fallen students and faculty. When she finished, the audience spontaneously took up a familiar chant: "Let's Go Hokies." In their moment of grief, it was a football cheer that best displayed the crowd's reaction to the horrors that had been experienced. For everyone there, the football chant allowed a release of emotion that was simultaneously bundled in tradition. It was a means to deal with pain through something that was familiar, something that would allow the members of the audience to be as one.

Much more than meaningless entertainment, sports—as New Yorkers displayed most poignantly in 2001, and the faculty and students of Virginia Tech demonstrated again in 2007—can provide solace, healing and solidarity for a community in crisis.

5

HALLOWED GROUNDS

OLYMPIA AND THE ANCIENT OLYMPICS

Countless young athletes the world over dream of one day participating in the modern Olympic Games. The Olympic ideal embodies the very peak of human physical achievement: to be the very best in the world and to bring honour to one's homeland. Every two years, hundreds of millions of people abandon their daily routines to watch the television coverage of the Olympics, but many fans have little knowledge of what the Olympic Games were like when they began thousands of years ago.

The ancient Olympic Games bore little resemblance to the Games of today. To begin with, they were intimately involved with Greek religion and the cult of physical perfection. Olympia, the venue of the Games, was home to the renowned Sanctuary of Zeus, which in turn housed a 13-metre (42-foot) statue of Zeus, seated on his throne with Nike, the goddess of victory, in his right hand. The statue was considered one of the Seven Wonders of the World. The Olympic

Torch also had religious overtones, as it commemorated the gift of fire to humanity by the Titan, Prometheus.

Only young, Greek-speaking men were allowed to compete (women competed in the separate, much-less prestigious Heraea Games, named for Hera, the wife of Zeus). The sporting events were conducted in the nude, and married women were not allowed even as spectators, on pain of death—it was considered inappropriate and shameful for a married woman to see any man, other than her husband, naked. Unmarried women were allowed to attend, since the possibility of marrying an Olympic champion was considered one of the highest goals to which a woman could aspire.

While today's Games include dozens of sports, the original Games were restricted to a single event, the *stadion* race, which varied from 180 to 240 metres (590 to 720 feet) in length. Interestingly, the modern word "stadium" derives from this Greek root. Contrary to popular belief, the marathon was never an event at the ancient Games. Over time, other sports were added to the Games, including a variety of different races, boxing, discus and javelin throwing, long jumping, wrestling, chariot racing, and the *pankration*. The *pankration* can perhaps best be compared to today's mixed martial arts competitions ... without the rules! Biting, eye-gouging and the breaking of bones were allowed. Athletes competed in the nude, and as such, rules against hitting "below the belt" did not (could not?) apply! Deaths were frequent.

A garland or wreath of olive leaves (symbolizing peace, and sacred to Zeus) was the ultimate "trophy" to which the ancient athletes could aspire. This modest accolade contrasts markedly with what modern Olympic champions can anticipate: many winning athletes can now look forward to lucrative commercial endorsement contracts, and a fast track into the high-paying world of professional sports.

Just as the olive wreath of victory symbolized peace, the ancient Games themselves were devoted to the concept of peaceful competition. All wars between the competing city states of ancient Greece would come to a temporary halt while the Games were in progress. Any warlike activity was regarded as sacrilegious, and the aggressors could face serious fines and expulsion from future games. Sadly, the modern Games lack this so-called "Olympic truce." Indeed, the Games themselves were cancelled during both the First and Second World Wars.

The ancient Olympic Games were held every four years in Olympia for almost 12 centuries. However, their association with pagan religious rituals would lead to their suppression in 393–94 CE (or, possibly, in 435 CE). The Roman emperor Theodosius I (or his grandson, Theodosius II), in an effort to impose Christianity throughout the empire, banned the Games. They would not reappear until the first of the modern Olympics was held—in Athens, Greece—in 1896.

Olympia, the site of the original Games, would be totally destroyed in a massive earthquake in the 6th century CE. However, although the site of the ancient competitions has long since vanished, Olympia itself continues to play an honoured role in the Olympic Games today. An integral part of the opening ceremony of the modern Games is the lighting of the Olympic Torch. The torch itself is ignited several months earlier, at Olympia, in Greece: the "birthplace" of sports.

MONTREAL FORUM

March 11, 1996, marked the end of an era. That night, the Montreal Canadiens defeated the Dallas Stars 4-1. To be sure, this was not the last time the fabled Canadiens would win a hockey game, but it *was* the night that the lights went out in the Montreal Forum.

The Forum! For millions of hockey fans across Canada, the very name conjures up visions of glory. From its opening game on November 29, 1924, through nearly 72 years, the Forum was home to some of the finest hockey ever seen. As the *Sporting News* would observe in 1996, the Forum was "the most storied building in hockey history."

Most people nowadays associate the Forum with the Montreal Canadiens, and it is understandable that they would do so. After all, in the 72 years that the Forum was open, the "Habs," as the Canadiens are known to their fans, would bring home the Stanley Cup—hockey's most coveted trophy—a total of 22 times (they were also Stanley Cup champions in 1915–16 and 1923–24, before the Forum opened). Altogether, 32 Stanley Cup final series were played in the Forum, and only two teams (New York Rangers in 1928, against the Montreal Maroons, and Calgary Flames in 1989, against the Canadiens) ever won the Cup when facing their opponents in front of a Forum crowd.

Skating into immortality on the Forum's centre ice were the Canadiens' legendary "Punch Line" (Maurice "Rocket" Richard, Toe Blake and Elmer Lach), which dominated the NHL in the 1950s; individual legends Jacques Plante, Jean Beliveau, Bernie "Boom Boom" Geoffrion, Guy Lafleur, Henri Richard, Ken Dryden, and Patrick Roy; and the mighty Canadiens' teams in the late 1950s that captured five consecutive Stanley Cups (1956–1960). So many, and sometimes so improbable, were the Canadiens' accomplishments that as the years went by, another kind of legend sprang up: that of the "Ghosts of the Forum." This legend would have it that ghosts of players past haunted the Forum, lending their beloved Canadiens a helping hand when required. One such occasion was May 10, 1979, when the Habs were playing the Boston Bruins in Game 7 of the semi-finals. The Bruins had not won a playoff series against Montreal since 1943, but that May evening, it looked as though the jinx was about to be lifted. Leading 4-3, with less than four minutes left, all the Boston team had to do was run out the clock. Then, disaster struck—the Bruins were penalized for having too many men on the ice! Montreal scored on the resulting power play and went on to win the game (and the series) in overtime. The Bruins, and their fans, were in shock. What had just happened? Did the ghost of some former Canadien great come through for his teammates, ensuring that a Boston player would stay on the ice a few seconds too long? Or was it just bad "puck luck"? We will never know, of course. But there are sports fans who had the good fortune to visit the Forum in its heyday who claim to have felt a certain,

FAST FACT

So iconic was the Forum in the minds of Canadians that it was unthinkable that the opening game of the legendary "Summit Series" between Canada and the Soviet Union—on September 2, 1972—could be held anywhere else. Unfortunately, the result of that game does not number amongst the finer moments in Forum history (from a Canadian standpoint, in any event), for the Soviets shocked the all-star Canadian team 7-3. (Canada would go on to win that series, but the opening game showed the players that they would have to fight for every victory.)

indefinable "something" in the air as they walked its hallowed halls. Ghosts, perhaps?

While the Forum and the Habs are inextricably linked in the minds of millions, the Forum was also home to the Montreal Maroons (National Hockey League), the Montreal Victorias and the Montreal Royals (Quebec Senior Hockey League), the Montreal Junior Canadiens (Quebec Junior Hockey League and Ontario Hockey Association/League), the Montreal Voyageurs (American Hockey League), and the Montreal Bleu Blanc Rouge and the Montreal Juniors (Quebec Major Junior Hockey League). The Montreal Maroons, who played in the NHL from 1924 until 1938, brought the Stanley Cup back to the Forum twice—in 1925–26 and again in 1934–35.

In addition to hockey, the Forum also briefly housed the Montreal Manic (North American Soccer League), and the Montreal Roadrunners, an inline hockey team (Roller Hockey International). It hosted scores of professional wrestling matches, numerous rock concerts, and was the site for five events in the 1976 Summer Olympics (gymnastics, handball, basketball, volleyball and boxing). At the time of its closure, the Forum had a total capacity of 17,959, of which some 1,600 were standing-room-only seats in the so-called "nosebleed" section. Over the course of seven decades, more than 90 million visitors would fill those seats—over a million a year.

Sadly, though, time stands still for no one ... and for no place. Despite its decades of greatness, even the mighty Forum could not go on forever. A modern, state-of-the-art facility with a greatly expanded seating capacity was required to take hockey in Montreal into the 21st century. Thus it was decided that the aging Forum would be replaced by the newly constructed Molson Centre (now the Bell Centre).

That last Canadiens game in the Forum was an unforgettable evening for all present. The Canadiens' team motto comes from the Robert Service poem "In Flanders Fields": "To you from failing hands we throw the torch; be yours to hold it high." At the end of the game Émile Bouchard, at 77 the oldest surviving former Canadiens captain, skated onto the ice carrying a symbolic torch, which was then passed on to each succeeding captain up to Pierre Turgeon, captain at the time. And, in perhaps the most touching moment of all, the spectators gave a 10-minute standing ovation to Maurice "the Rocket" Richard, one of the greatest Canadiens of all time—there was barely a dry eye in the house.

Today the Forum has been reinvented as a downtown entertainment centre known as the Pepsi Forum, but echoes of its past glory can still be found, including a statue of "Rocket" Richard, a bronze Montreal Canadiens logo surrounded by 24 Stanley Cup banners, and original seats scattered throughout the complex... Ghosts of the Forum, indeed.

MADISON SQUARE GARDEN

Think fast: What do Muhammad Ali, Jumbo the Elephant, Billy Graham, Marilyn Monroe, and the New York Knickerbockers all have in common? Give up? Well, at one time or another, each was the centre of attention at Madison Square Garden.

Nothing says "The Big Apple" like "The Garden" (also known as "MSG"), and in many ways, Madison Square Garden has the same significance to Americans as the Montreal Forum had for Canadians. The Garden, which has been in operation for more than 130 years, has, in fact, had four incarnations. The original, 10,000-seat MSG, on 26th Street and Madison Avenue, was constructed in 1879 (operating until 1890) by none other than P.T. ("There's a sucker born every minute") Barnum, of circus fame—hence the appearance of Jumbo the Elephant at the Garden (in 1882).

The second building, designed by renowned architect Stanford White, opened in 1890. It had a seating capacity of

8,000 and, because of its unique, Beaux Arts design, immediately became a New York landmark. MSG II, as it has since been called, hosted hundreds of memorable events over its 35-year history, including, on December 14, 1920, the only indoor bout of Jack Dempsey's career. But this incarnation of The Garden was never a financial success, and in 1925 it was closed. Not only was it closed, but a decision was made to move to a more advantageous site: on 8th Avenue, between 49th and 50th Streets.

Remarkably, the third version of Madison Square Garden was constructed in less than a year, with the ground-breaking ceremony held on January 9 and the official opening on December 15, 1925. The new arena had a maximum capacity of 18,496, and had significantly better access to the city's mass-transit system than its predecessors. Home to the New York Rangers and the short-lived New York Americans of the NHL, and the New York Knickerbockers ("the Knicks") of the NBA, the presence of professional sports teams would greatly enhance the profitability of the site. The Rangers would bring the Stanley Cup to The Garden three times; the Americans, on the other hand, had trouble making the playoffs and never managed to bring home a championship banner.

The Garden would be home to many other events in addition to hockey and basketball. In 1938, more than 15,000 fans gathered to watch figure skater (and actress) Sonia Henie and her travelling show, the Hollywood Ice Review. Evangelist Billy Graham preached to spellbound crowds every night for an incredible 16 consecutive weeks in 1957. But the moment which stands out for many as the ultimate performance in Madison Square Garden took place on May 29, 1962. That night, Marilyn Monroe crooned out her sultry version of "Happy Birthday" to then president John F. Kennedy.

Six years after the last echoes of Marilyn's voice had faded away, The Garden would have its fourth (and latest) incarnation, opening in 1968. Now situated on 8th Avenue between 31st and 33rd Streets, the present MSG has a seating capacity of between 18,000 and 21,000, depending on the event. The Garden continues to house the Rangers and the Knicks, as well as the New York Liberty (of the Women's

National Basketball Association); other teams have come and gone over the years.

Madison Square Garden hosts, on average, 320 events a year and is believed by many performers to have the best acoustics—and the best fans—in the world. Elton John has played there a record 60 times, including for his 60th birthday on March 25, 2007. John Lennon made his final concert appearance there, on November 28, 1974. Some of these events have been classics, such as the first Muhammad Ali–Joe Frazier match-up—the so-called "Fight of the Century"—on March 8, 1971 (Ali lost). Others have been perhaps less classic, but nonetheless memorable, such as the first WrestleMania, held on March 31, 1985; has anyone ever recovered from the sight of guest timekeeper Liberace dancing the can-can with the New York City Rockettes in front of 19,121 cheering spectators?

This list could go on indefinitely, but suffice to say that Madison Square Garden is widely considered to be the world's greatest entertainment complex. The environment, the history, the crowds: all combine to make The Garden one of the most iconic sports venues in the world.

WIMBLEDON

"Take heed" ... "Watch out" ... or, more inelegantly, "DUCK!!" These are all more-or-less literal translations of the French word *tenez*, from which we get the modern English word "tennis." The French connection is relatively easy to explain, since the earliest documented forms of tennis can be traced back to twelfth-century France. Like the golfer calling out "Fore!" before completing his stroke, "*tenez*" was a warning from the server to the receiver.

During the Hundred Years War (1337–1453), the English occupied large sections of France, and it is at this time that the game first appeared in England. It quickly became popular with royalty (Henry VIII was an avid player), and the regal connection has continued ever since, so that tennis, like polo, is often referred to as "the sport of kings."

To be sure, the game as played by Henry VIII in medieval times bore little resemblance to tennis as we know it today.

The modern form of tennis only appeared in 1874, after a Major Walter C. Wingfield examined the various forms of outdoor racquet sports being played in England, and came up with a codified set of rules and equipment, for which he then took out a patent. Major Wingfield turned out to be the right man with the right idea at the right time, and his new game was an immediate hit. A mere three years later, in 1877, the "All England Croquet and Lawn Tennis Club" was formed. In July of that year, the club organized its first tournament, and "the Wimbledon Championships" were born. Twenty-two players (all men) participated, and Spencer Gore emerged as the first "Gentlemen's Singles" Wimbledon champion. Gore played his final match in front of a grand total of 200 spectators—a far cry from modern attendance levels. In 1884, women were allowed to participate for the first time, and Maud Watson emerged as the first "Ladies' Singles" champion from a field of 13 competitors.

The long association between tennis and the monarchy in England came to focus on the Wimbledon Championships in particular over a century ago, in 1907, when the Prince of Wales (later Edward VII) attended for the first time. He was offered, and accepted, the Presidency of the club—a position that has been held by a member of the Royal Family ever since; the current president is the Duke of Kent, who is a cousin of the Queen. Since 1910, the ruling monarch has been known as a "Patron of the Club."

As one might expect from an event held in Britain—home of the Changing of the Guard, fish and chips, and the "stiff

FAST FACT

There is one long-standing Wimbledon "tradition" of which the home crowd is probably not fond: the English seem to consistently lose on their own ground. The last English woman to win the Singles title was Virginia Wade, in 1977. The men are doing even worse—an English man has not won the Singles ever since Fred Perry in 1936!

upper lip"— the Wimbledon Championships have developed many traditions over the years. To begin with, of course, Wimbledon has long been associated with the eating of strawberries and cream. Popular legend has it that King George V first introduced the treat to the crowds—another royal connection. However, it is more likely that the tradition simply developed over time, since both tennis and strawberries are associated with spring in England. Whatever the case may be, every year, spectators go through a staggering amount of the dessert: over 28,000 kilograms (62,000 pounds/31 tons) of strawberries and almost 6,000 litres (1,300 gallons) of cream!

Another tradition: white is definitely "in" at Wimbledon ... but why? Well, it is because the club has never seen fit to abandon its very strict dress code, despite the fact that such rules have been relaxed at other tennis Grand Slam events. All players must check with club officials before they can wear a new outfit to the tournament, and while a little colour is now allowed, players must ensure that they are wearing mainly white ... or they don't play! Wimbledon is also known for its ball boys and ball girls (BBGs, for short). However, in stark contrast to the often brilliant white outfits worn by the players, BBGs are supposed to be as unobtrusive as possible. As such, their uniforms were traditionally green, so that they could blend into the background; in 2006, these were changed to navy blue and cream (cream again?!).

Steeped as it is in tradition, and now drawing up to half a million spectators annually—not to mention the millions of fans who watch the televised matches—Wimbledon has become one of the greatest, and most iconic, venues associated with professional sports.

INDIANAPOLIS MOTOR SPEEDWAY

O f all the world's iconic sporting facilities, the largest is unquestionably the Indianapolis Motor Speedway at 559 acres, or 2.3 square kilometres. It also has the world's greatest seating capacity, with 257,325 permanent seats; with infield seating, this number can rise to some 400,000! The Speedway is best known as the home of the celebrated Indianapolis 500-Mile Race—the Indy 500, as it is more commonly known. The Indy 500 has been dubbed the greatest spectacle in racing by aficionados of the sport, and is one of the events in the so-called "Triple Crown" of motorsports, along with the 24 Hours of Le Mans, and the Monaco Grand Prix. Since 1994, the Speedway has also been home to the Brickyard 400—the most highly attended event on the NASCAR circuit, with annual crowds of more than a quarter of a million.

In the early years of the 20th century, sports car racing was in its infancy, and early races were held on either public roads or horse tracks. These were not designed for speed racing, however, and accidents were common. Furthermore, spectators had only a fleeting glimpse of the vehicles whizzing by at the then unprecedented speeds of 50–60 miles per hour. Then along came Carl Graham Fisher. Fisher was an Indianapolis businessman who had made a fortune in vehicle parts and highway construction, and the Indianapolis Speedway was his brainchild.

Construction began on March 15, 1909, and the site opened on August 12, 1909. However, the original track, made of crushed stone and tar, was in service for a mere three days before management deemed it too dangerous for racing. In order to fix the problem, 3.2 million paving bricks were set and mortared in place (the final brick was made of gold and was laid in place by Indiana's governor at the time, Thomas Marshall). As a result, the Speedway became colloquially known as "The Brickyard."

Unfortunately, the bricks proved to be no match for improving technology, and as racing speeds steadily increased (in 1925, Peter DePaolo became the first driver to average 100 miles per hour at the Indy 500), the track once again became dangerous. In a four-year period, from 1931 until 1935, fifteen people died at the Speedway, mainly because of dangerous track conditions. In 1937 the site's owners began replacing the bricks with asphalt. The bricks were not discarded, however, and in a nod to tradition, the start/finish line is still paved with bricks. The line is three feet wide, and is known as "The Brickyard." As these bricks wear down, they are replaced with others from the original track.

The Indy 500, the race for which the Speedway is best known, began in 1911. The inaugural race on May 30 saw Ray Harroun, driving the "Marmon Wasp," emerge victorious from a pack of 40 contenders. The qualifying speed for the race was 75 miles per hour, and Harroun's average speed for the race was 74.6 mph, in a winning time of 6:42:08. Harroun was the first driver to use a single-seated vehicle, and he was the first to use a rear-view mirror.

The high speeds involved in car racing mean that, throughout its history, fatalities at the Indianapolis Speedway, while unfortunate, have not been uncommon. In fact, on August 19, 1909, only a week after the Speedway opened, five people met their fate. The dubious honour of being the first fatality at the Speedway belongs to a Canadian, Wilfred

FAST FACT

The first race held at the Indianapolis Speedway had nothing to do with cars; rather, it was a race between helium balloons. On June 5, 1909, 40,000 spectators watched as nine balloons lifted off and soon drifted out of sight (the winning balloon was Universal City).

Bourque. Bourque's mechanic, Harry Halcomb, tapped him on the shoulder during the race to warn him that another car was approaching. As Bourque glanced back, he apparently hit a rut. The car flipped over, and both he and Halcomb were killed. In a separate accident later in the day, another mechanic and two spectators died.

Over the years, the death toll at the Indianapolis Speedway has steadily climbed. A total of 41 drivers have been killed—14 at the Indy 500 race itself, and 27 others in practice runs or other races. As well, 14 mechanics and 7 spectators have been killed at the Indy since 1909.

In the intervening century, there have been many other memorable races at the Speedway, but two in particular stand out. In 1992, Al Unser, Jr. defeated Scott Goodyear by the closest margin ever recorded at the track: a mere 0.043 seconds—talk about a photo finish! And in 2005, a gender barrier of sorts was broken, when Danica Patrick became the first woman ever to lead the Indy 500, although she finished fourth overall. Patrick's achievement is all the more impressive since only seven women have qualified since 1971, the year in which women were allowed to participate for the first time.

6

SUPERHUMAN FEATS

FLOAT LIKE A BUTTERFLY, STING LIKE A BEE

In January 1975, British singer Johnny Wakelin rose to the top of the record charts with his hit song "Black Superman." Amongst other memorable lines was this one: "Float like a butterfly, sting like a bee," a phrase that Mohammed Ali had coined to describe his own boxing style.

Ali is generally regarded as one of the best boxers of all time—although he would probably dispute the words "one of," since he prefers to refer to himself simply as "The Greatest"— but few recall Ali's beginnings as a fighter. Do you? Well, the story goes like this...

It was 1954, in Louisville, Kentucky, and 12-year-old Cassius Marcellus Clay was furious. Someone had stolen his bicycle. He reported the theft to a cop by the name of Joe Martin, saying that he was going to "whup" whoever had stolen his bike. Martin, who was also a boxing instructor, gave the youngster some sage advice: "Well you'd better learn to fight before you start challenging people that you're gonna whup."

Young Cassius Clay would do exactly that. He took lessons from Martin when he could and, determined to become more nimble on his feet, asked his brother Rudy to throw rocks at him in their yard, which he would attempt to dodge. According to Rudy Clay, Cassius managed to dodge every rock, every time. No matter how many rocks Rudy threw at him, Cassius already seemed able to "float like a butterfly." At the age of 18, Clay won the gold medal in the Light Heavyweight category at the 1960 Rome Olympics. Although he would later throw the medal away after being refused service at a "whites only" restaurant in his home town of Louisville, his remarkable boxing career was underway.

Occurring as it did in the context of the American civil rights movement and the war in Vietnam, Cassius Clay's career as a boxer was often overshadowed by his political views. He was drawn to the African-American religious movement known as the "Nation of Islam," which advocated radical policies such as a separate nation for Black Americans. After his 1964 victory over Sonny Liston for the heavyweight title, Clay danced around the ring shouting "I'm the greatest! I shook up the world!" Soon after, he announced his conversion to Islam, and changed his name to Mohammed Ali. It was a deeply unpopular thing to do. Ali also refused to serve in Vietnam, on religious grounds, declaring that "I ain't got no quarrel with them Vietcong... No Vietcong ever called me Nigger." He was stripped of his title, fined, and sentenced to prison—although he never actually served time.

By 1971, public opinion in the United States began turning against the Vietnam War, and Ali was allowed to fight again. What followed would be three of the most memorable bouts of all time. The "Fight of the Century" on March 8, 1971, pitted Ali against champion Joe Frazier—it resulted in the first professional loss of Ali's career. The "Fight of the Century" was followed by the "Rumble in the Jungle." On October 30, 1974, in Kinshasa, Zaire, Ali regained his title, defeating George Foreman (who had earlier beaten Joe Frazier). It was this match that inspired Wakelin to write "Black Superman." The "Rumble in the Jungle" was followed by the "Thrilla in Manila," on October 1, 1975, a rematch against Joe Frazier. Ali took the bout in 15 rounds.

Ali would lose his title in February 1978 to Leon Spinks, before winning it back, for the last time, in a rematch on

FAST FACT

In March 1975, Ali faced off against a little-known boxer named Chuck Wepner. Wepner proved a tough opponent, knocking Ali down before finally losing the bout in the fifteenth round. Their match-up would inspire the movie *Rocky*.

September 15 that year. He retired for the first time in 1979, attempted a comeback in 1980, and retired permanently in 1981. In 1984 he was diagnosed with Parkinson's Disease—an ailment to which boxers are highly susceptible, because of their frequent head trauma.

In later years, the positions that Ali had taken in the 1960s and 1970s on the civil rights movement and the Vietnam War would be largely vindicated. Few today would maintain that segregation was a reasonable policy, or that the conflict in Vietnam was a just war, and Ali's stock has risen with the passage of time. In 1999, *Sports Illustrated* named Ali the "Sportsman of the Century."

Nowadays, few people can name the world boxing champion, apart from fans of the sport. This was never the case with Ali: he dominated the media and the world of boxing like no other champion before, or since, and virtually everyone knows his name. Perhaps, as he says himself, Mohammed Ali is, quite simply, "The Greatest."

And it all started with the theft of a bicycle.

GOLDEN OLDIE

G enerally speaking, the world of sports belongs to the young—most professional athletes retire at some time in their thirties, if they aren't forced out by injuries before that. Olympic competition is dominated by athletes in their twenties; in certain sports, such as women's gymnastics, competitors in their teens seem to dominate. But there are also individuals who have defied this generalizion, not only competing, but excelling, in their sport into their forties and fifties. For instance, at age 45, George Foreman won the IBF and WBA heavyweight titles, defeating then-champion Michael Moorer, who was 19 years his junior. Gordie Howe scored 15 goals in his last season in the NHL, at the age of 51—many of Howe's team-mates had not even been born when "Mr. Hockey" skated his first professional game. And it took 35-year-old Stewart Cink a four-hole playoff to beat 59-year-old Tom Watson for the British Open golf title in 2009.

Among the more remarkable of these true sports legends is Jack Nicklaus, "The Golden Bear," one of the greatest golfers of all time.

Jack Nicklaus was born on January 21, 1940, and entered the pro ranks at the end of 1961. For the next two decades, he dominated the world of golf, racking up a total of 17 major championships, including five Masters titles (1963, 1965, 1966, 1972 and 1975). However, it was championship number 18 that was the sweetest, because that was the tournament commentators said he couldn't possibly win.

In 1986, Nicklaus was 46 years old. Too old, according to many, to even consider entering the Masters Championship that year. Tom McCollister, for one, opined in the *Atlanta Journal-Constitution* that The Golden Bear was "done, washed up, through." Nicklaus clipped out the article and posted it on his refrigerator.

Despite the risk of being humiliated in a competition that he had so often dominated in the past, Nicklaus decided to enter the Masters that year. As he himself said: "I'm not as good as I was 15 years ago. [But] just occasionally I want to be as good as I once was." He joined the field of forty-eight players who teed off on April 10, 1986. The Golden Bear was the second oldest of the group (Lee Trevino was six weeks older than Nicklaus!). Most of the other players were at least a decade younger.

For the first three days Nicklaus surprised many of the spectators by exceeding expectations, perhaps even his own. On April 13, the last day of the tournament, Nicklaus was four shots off the lead, with only four holes left to play. It was a respectable performance, but a far cry from the way he had dominated the field in his five previous Masters wins. Nicklaus was close to admitting that the years had taken too big a toll: "Walking up the fairways on the last few holes, I had tears in my eyes four or five times. I just welled up. But then I told myself, 'Hey, you've got golf to play'."

And play golf he did! To the astonishment of the crowd, the commentators, and the other players, The Golden Bear rallied for one last charge. He shot an eagle and two birdies to finish the final round with a remarkable 7-under-par 65. Six birdies and the eagle over the final 10 holes gave him 9-under 279 and a one-stroke victory over Greg Norman and Tom Kite, both in their thirties. Jack Nicklaus had won his sixth Masters championship, and at age 46 he was (and remains) the oldest golfer to have done so. Nobody could blame Nicklaus for exulting: "This may be as fine a round of golf as I ever played, particularly those last 10 holes." After all, it was an astonishing performance for someone who was "done, washed up, through."

Then came the sweetest moment of all. Tom McCollister was among the journalists in the post-tournament interview room. McCollister's column had niggled away at The Golden Bear, especially because he worried that it might be true. As he said, "Tell you the truth, I kind of agreed with Tom, I'm afraid, but it helped get me going." The two men's eyes met, and McCollister smiled and said, "Glad I could help."

HIS AIRNESS

oca-Cola. Nike. Boxers or briefs? When pondering great sports moments these may not be words that leap to mind but if you put them beside a 6'6" basketball star, all of that changes. While his many commercial endorsements have made him one of the most recognizable faces in sport, Michael Jordan is also arguably the greatest basketball player ever to grace the court.

Michael Jeffrey Jordan was born on January 17, 1963, in Brooklyn, New York, but moved to North Carolina with his family as a child. From an early age, young Michael loved sports, playing baseball, football, and basketball. But when he tried out for his high school basketball team in the tenth grade, he was deemed too short, and failed to make the cut. Fortunately, the next summer Michael started growing, adding an additional 7" over the next two years, and finally stopping at 6'6". After that, he had no problem making the cut, and earned a basketball scholarship to the University of North Carolina.

It didn't take long for Michael to make an impression, and on November 28, 1983, he made the cover of *Sports Illustrated* while still in college—he would grace the cover an additional 50 times over the next 20 years!

In 1984, Michael was drafted by the Chicago Bulls of the NBA. On December 10 that year, the *Sports Illustrated* cover proclaimed that "A Star is Born," and so he was. In his rookie season he had a 51.5% success rate when aiming for the basket. That's right, more than one out of every two shots that Jordan took made it through the hoops. No other newcomer could match him, and he capped his freshman season by being voted "Rookie of the Year."

He made it look easy. So easy, in fact that he was dubbed "Air Jordan" and "His Airness," because at times it seemed as though he—and the basketball—were defying gravity, literally hanging in the air while other mere mortals were earthbound. And the basketballs just kept on dropping through the hoop: altogether, "His Airness" had a career total of 32,292 points—an average of more than 30 points per game.

With Jordan on their squad, the Chicago Bulls were a force to be reckoned with throughout the 1990s, winning six NBA championships over the course of the decade: "three-peats" in 1991, 1992, 1993, and again in 1996, 1997, 1998. (The Bulls have not won a championship since "Air Jordan" retired.)

Jordan's dominance of the courts was so complete that in addition to the six NBA championships, he was named the NBA's "Most Valuable Player" five times (one in every four years of his career). He was an All-Star 14 times and made it to the All-NBA "First Team" 10 times. To top things off, "Air Jordan" played on two gold-medal winning Olympic teams for the United States, in 1984 and 1992.

Following the first "three-peat" with the Bulls, Michael Jordan suddenly announced his retirement. His father had been brutally murdered that summer, and his heart was no longer in the game. However, champion that he was, Jordan overcame his personal grief and in 1995 he returned to the game that he loved, helping his team to its second "three-peat" before retiring again in early 1999.

There was one more comeback left in Jordan, and in 2001, at the age of 38, he signed on with the Washington Wizards, donating his salary that year to the relief effort following the terrorist attacks of September 11, 2001. The years—and the injuries—were catching up, however, and "His Airness" retired for the final time in 2003, leaving millions of fans with fond memories of his aerodynamic performances on the basketball court.

Perhaps more than any other player, Michael Jordan became the "face" of basketball to the world. In the words of another basketball great, Earvin "Magic" Johnson, "There's Michael Jordan and then there is the rest of us."

THE OLYMPIC LIGHTNING BOLT

He was christened Usain St. Leo, but nowadays, most people just call him "Lightning Bolt." He is, of course, Jamaica's pride and joy, Usain Bolt, the "world's fastest man." The title is an unofficial one, but the general consensus is that it belongs to whoever wins the 100-metre sprint at the Summer Olympic Games. In 2008, Usain Bolt seized the title, and he did it in style.

"Lightning Bolt" burst upon the racing scene at the 2002 World Junior Championships where, at the age of 16, he thrilled the home-town audience by winning a gold medal in the 200-metre race. In doing so, he also became the youngest-ever gold medalist in that competition. It was Usain's first gold medal, but it would not be his last: far from it.

Fast forward to August 16, 2008, in Beijing, China. Eight men took their places at the starting line for the all-important 100-metre race. Standing at 6'5", Usain towered over his rivals. However, it was not only his height, but also his speed, that truly set him apart from the others ... that, and maybe his Puma Theseus II golden spike shoes—their colour a definite omen of things to come.

When the starter's pistol fired, "Lightning Bolt" practically flew out of the blocks and surged to the head of the pack, increasing his lead with every stride. So solid was his lead, in fact, that with 10 metres to go he began to decelerate. His confidence was justified, for not only did Usain win the race, but he set a new world record in doing so: 9.69 seconds. Experts calculated that his record time could have been even lower—9.55 seconds—had he not started to slow down.

Four days later, on August 20, the "Lightning Bolt" was back in the starting blocks: this time for the 200-metre race. It was a different race, but it yielded the same result. Usain and his golden shoes surged into the lead, a lead so great that the cameramen had difficulty keeping the other racers in the shot. This time, though, Usain didn't slow down. He ran hard, and when he crossed the finish line, he shattered another world record, with a winning time of 19.30 seconds— more than half a second ahead of his nearest rival. When the anthems finished playing, and the medal presentation was over, "Lightning Bolt" returned to the Athletes' Village with his second gold medal of the Games.

But there was still more to come. On August 22, the 4 × 100-metre relay race was held, and "Lightning Bolt" was again one of the runners, this time as the third leg of the Jamaican team. The Jamaicans set a new world record of

37.10 seconds in taking the gold—almost a full second ahead of the silver medallists.

Taking three Olympic gold medals in track events is a fairly impressive tally by any standard. Indeed, the last man to do so was the great Carl Lewis, in 1984. However, Usain's achievement was even more incredible, in that he set a new world record for each event—he remains the only person in Olympic history to have done so.

It looks like the sky just might be the limit for "Lightning Bolt," for the records have continued to fall. In March 2009, at the Manchester Great City Games, he won the 150-metre race in 14.35 seconds. Later that year, and evidently competing against himself, Usain Bolt broke both his 100-metre and 200-metre Olympic records when racing at the World Championships in Berlin, with 9.58 and 19.19 seconds, respectively. Bolt's speed was so impressive that one-time Olympic champion Shawn Crawford commented, "Just coming out there...I felt like I was in a video game, that guy was moving—fast."

Whatever the future holds, it is likely to be quite some time before anyone beats the 2008 performance of Usain St. Leo Bolt—the Olympic "Lightning Bolt."

7 PROS WHO CON

FATHER KNOWS BEST?

In 2001, Danny Almonte was a pitching sensation. His fastball was clocked at over 70 miles per hour—the equivalent of a major league pitcher lobbing one over home plate at more than 90 mph. It was a remarkable accomplishment for a 12-year-old, and he was the talk of that year's Little League World Series. Danny had seemingly come out of nowhere, for he had barely been in the United States for a year before he burst upon the Little League scene.

Born in the Dominican Republic, Danny had moved to the United States in the year 2000 to join his father. Felipe Almonte loved baseball, and had started a baseball league for young players in the Dominican before moving to New York. Once Danny arrived, Felipe immediately registered him in "the Baby Bombers," a Little League team playing in the Bronx. Felipe believed his son was destined for baseball greatness, and it wasn't long before Danny became one of the stars of the team.

A big, strong kid, Danny stood 5'9" tall—taller than his head coach, and well above the average for 12-year-olds. But it was the strength and breadth of his pitching that was truly astonishing: he had mastered the fastball, changeup, curveball and slider. In addition, he had a unique pitching style, with a high leg kick that seemed to lend additional speed to his pitch. Baseball scouts from across the United States were paying careful attention to the newcomer.

The 2001 Little League World Series was a round-robin event, and Danny was victorious in the three games he

FAST FACT

Danny Almonte never made it to the Majors, instead playing with a variety of semi-pro teams. In 2010, he returned to the Bronx, where he coached his high school baseball team. Presumably, he exhibited better sportsmanship than his father. And what about **Matthew Cerda**, the 4'10" batter who cried when Danny struck him out? Matthew eventually grew to be 5'9" (the same height Danny had been in 2001)—and he *did* make it to the big leagues: in 2008 Matthew Cerda was drafted by the Chicago Cubs.

pitched. He struck out 62 of the 72 batters who faced him; at least one player, 4'10" dynamo Matthew Cerda, cried out of sheer frustration and embarrassment when he was struck out at Danny's hands for the third time. One of Danny's games was a no-hitter and another was a one-hit shutout. But most amazingly, Danny pitched a "perfect game"—meaning that no opposing player made it to base, or, in "baseballese," the opposition was "27 up, 27 down." It was the first perfect game in a Little League World Series since 1957. Felipe Almonte beamed with pride.

Danny's team lost the series in the championship game to a team from Florida, but that was not Danny's fault. Under Little League rules, he wasn't allowed to pitch in the final game, since he had pitched a complete game the day before. Nevertheless, "the Baby Bombers" became the darlings of New York. They were guests of honour at a Yankees game, and New York mayor Rudy Giuliani presented the team with the keys to the city. Danny and his dad were on top of the world—but not for long.

Danny's imposing physical stature had raised suspicions. Some of the adults involved with other teams had noticed what looked suspiciously like facial hair on Danny. He also appeared to have an Adam's apple. And he seemed to be interested in girls! Strange. Two of the other Little League teams hired some private investigators to find out what was up.

Of course, facial hair, an Adam's apple, and interest in girls—while unusual for 12-year-olds—are fairly commonplace for 14-year-olds, which was Danny's real age. Felipe

Almonte had cheated, forging Danny's birth certificate so that it would seem his son was born in 1989; an investigation in the Dominican Republic revealed that the boy was really born two years earlier, in 1987.

Danny and his team had to forfeit their winning games, and the adults involved were chastised by George W. Bush. Felipe Almonte was banned from participating in Little League baseball for the rest of his life. Poor Danny, who spoke no English at the time, was unaware of the forgery and was cleared of wrongdoing. He was the innocent victim of his father's ambition. Jim Caple, of ESPN TV, said that Felipe Almonte represented "the worst stereotype of the Little League Parent sprung to life."

SKATING WARS

Virtually every successful athlete has a strong competitive instinct. Without this, it would be difficult, if not impossible, to summon the reserves of strength and determination which are essential if one is to follow a rigorous training routine. It is this instinct which allows each athlete to achieve his—or her—personal best, and for most athletes, a personal best is satisfaction enough. Not so for Tonya Harding, an American figure skater who was determined to do whatever it took to compete in the 1994 Winter Olympics in Lillehammer, Norway.

Harding was an exceptionally talented skater. In 1991, she had clinched the American women's figure skating title, and went on to finish second in the world championships that year. She was also the first American female figure skater—and only the second female skater in the world—to finish a triple Axel jump in a competitive figure skating event. This remarkable feat involves the skater rotating in the air

3.5 times before landing on the ice. Unfortunately, it is Harding's very talent that makes her story such a disgrace.

Another talented young American figure skater, Nancy Kerrigan, was competing at the same time and in many of the same events as Tonya Harding. In 1991, Kerrigan had finished third in the U.S. championships—the same event in which Harding had finished first. But in 1993, it was Kerrigan who took first place in the event, while Harding came in fourth. The stage was now set for the shameful events leading up to the Lillehammer Games.

In 1994, the U.S. championships were being held in Detroit, and the performances of the competitors would be instrumental in the selection of the U.S. women's Olympic figure skating team. Apparently feeling that her own considerable talents were insufficient to defeat Kerrigan, Tonya Harding decided to take matters into her own hands—or rather, to place them in the hands of her ex-husband, Jeff Gillooly, and her bodyguard, Shawn Eric Eckardt. The three conspired to ensure that Kerrigan would be unable to skate her way to Olympic glory, and two further individuals—Derrick B. Smith and Shane Stant—were drawn into plot. Stated bluntly, Stant was hired to break Kerrigan's knee and end her skating career, while Smith was to drive the get-away car.

The vicious attack took place on January 6, 1994. Stant had originally looked for Kerrigan at her regular rink in Massachusetts, but finding that she had already left for the U.S. championships, he followed her to Detroit. There, he attacked her off-ice, attempting to break her knee with a collapsible metal baton. Fortunately for Kerrigan, Stant was off-target, striking her on the thigh a few inches above the knee. Nevertheless, he succeeded in doing enough damage to force Kerrigan to withdraw from the competition. It seemed as though Harding's scheme would be successful, since she won the event. Both Kerrigan and Harding were named to the U.S. Women's Olympic team.

The plot quickly unravelled, and along with it, Tonya Harding's career. Her cohorts were charged, and all served prison time. An attempt was made to remove Harding from the Olympic team, but she threatened legal action, stating that she had not (yet) been convicted of a crime. The media coverage of Harding at Lillehammer threatened to overshadow the reporting on the Games themselves, but when all was said and done, Nancy Kerrigan recovered sufficiently from her injury to give the performance of her career, and won the Silver Medal. Harding finished in eighth spot, well out of the medal standings. Harding had sacrificed her reputation, and her career, for nothing.

In the aftermath of the fiasco, Tonya Harding managed to avoid a jail sentence by pleading guilty to attempting to hinder the prosecution of the offenders. She was given three years' probation, a substantial fine, and ordered to perform community service. She was also stripped of her 1994 U.S. title, and banned for life from participating in the U.S. Figure Skating Association.

Harding's subsequent career became a parody of itself. She was involved in an escalating series of run-ins with the law, many alcohol-related, and more than a few of them suspicious, if not downright spurious. In an attempt to capitalize on her reputation, she launched a boxing "career" in 2002, with Fox TV's *Celebrity Boxing*. Two years later, after six bouts, she retired. In her 2008 autobiography, *The Tonya Tapes*, Harding denied that she had been involved in the attack on Nancy Kerrigan, but her protestations of innocence have been greeted with scepticism.

In 2008, Harding became a regulator commentator on *TruTV Presents: World's Dumbest...* Somehow, that seems appropriate.

As for Nancy Kerrigan, she was inducted into the United States Figure Skating Hall of Fame in 2004, ten years after her silver medal-winning performance in Lillehammer.

THE
SHORTCUT

I t had taken Rosie only 2:31:56 to complete the Boston Marathon! Not only was it a new women's record for the Boston race, her time was also the third-fastest for any woman running a marathon, anywhere. All in all, it was a remarkable achievement. Through sheer determination, Rosie Ruiz had risen from her humble origins as a refugee from Castro's Cuba to capture her share of the American Dream.

It was April 21, 1980, and the 84th annual Boston Marathon was drawing to a close. More than 20,000 runners had started the race that day, but only a few would share the honour of standing on the winner's podium. Beaming with pride, 27-year-old Rosie Ruiz was among those select few, sporting a green laurel wreath atop her head and the first-place gold medal around her neck. She had shaved an astonishing 25 minutes off of her running time in the New York Marathon the previous year, and had finished more than three minutes ahead of her nearest female competitor, Canadian Jacqueline Gareau. And Rosie made it all look so easy—why, she had barely broken into a sweat!

Hmmm ... no sweating? After running 26 miles in record time? Especially when she was wearing a heavy t-shirt, which was hardly standard marathon attire? Suspicions began to surface almost immediately about "Rosie's Run." One of the most suspicious individuals was second-place finisher Jacqueline Gareau, who was certain that she had been one of the lead runners since the beginning of the Marathon. Gareau could not recall having seen Rosie pass her during the run. Neither could third-place finisher, Patti Lyons (who incidentally had set a new American women's record of 2:35:08!).

When a reporter asked if she was inspired by the female students of Wellesley College—who annually gather to cheer on female runners—Rosie did not recall seeing them. Nor did the Wellesley students remember having seen Rosie. How odd! The video cameras didn't appear to be working either, as none of them had captured Rosie on film. In fact, only two people *could* recall having seen Rosie during the race: John Faulkner and Sola Mahoney. The problem was that they saw her when she quietly emerged from among the spectators about half a mile from the finish line. Rosie, it appeared, had taken a shortcut!

It would take eight long days before the entire story came out, but in the meantime a photographer by the name of Susan Morrow recalled meeting Rosie a year earlier at the time of the New York Marathon. The trouble was... Morrow met Rosie *on the subway*. They chatted, and Morrow accompanied Rosie from the subway to the race, at which point they separated. Rosie went on to the first aid clinic, where she reported a sore ankle and a finishing time of 2:56:29!

What had happened? Well, although no one actually saw her on the Boston subway, the fact that no one saw her in the race, either, coupled with the fact that she had hopped aboard the subway during the New York Marathon, weighed heavily against Rosie. A week later, she was disqualified, and Jacqueline Gareau was declared the victor. The only mystery remaining is: What did Rosie actually *do* during those "missing two hours"? To this day, she maintains that she ran the entire race.

The victors in athletic competitions often benefit from corporate endorsements, or go on to become media stars in their own right. After her disqualification, none of these offers would come Rosie's way, although with tongue firmly in cheek, David Kindred of the *Washington Post* suggested that she start her own line of racing footwear: "Rosie Ruiz shoes—so comfortable that when the marathon is over your feet feel like they've only gone a mile or two." Instead, Rosie opted for a career in real estate, where two years after the marathon fiasco, she was arrested for embezzling her employers.

Although she was a cheater, Rosie nevertheless did contribute to the sport of marathon competitions: her legacy can be found in the computerized chips that are now placed on runners' shoes, and the much-improved camera surveillance, which records the starting and finishing times of runners at various checkpoints. It is unlikely that there will ever be another "Rosie's Run."

8

PAVING THE WAY

"OWEN"-ING
THE PODIUM

Adolf Hitler had high hopes for the 1936 Summer Olympic Games. They were to be held in Berlin, and marked the first time the Games were hosted by Germany. Hitler intended to make the Olympics his showcase to the world. The Games, he believed, would demonstrate the superiority of the Nazi philosophy, and would highlight the remarkable progress Germany had made since the Nazis had come to power a mere three years earlier.

Germany's Olympic team consisted of "Aryan" (White, and non-Jewish) athletes only. Hitler was confident that they would dominate the Games, and to a certain degree, he was right. The German team finished first overall, with a tally of 33 gold, 26 silver and 30 bronze medals (for a total of 89). In second place was the team from the United States, taking home 24 gold, 20 silver and 12 bronze medals (56 in total).

While the German team as a whole dominated the 1936 Games, a single American athlete stole the Olympic spotlight that year, taking a record four gold medals in track and field events (100 and 200 metre sprints, long jump, and four-man 100-metre relay). That athlete was none other than Jesse Owens, one of the greatest Olympic athletes of all time. And Owens' success was a particular problem for the Nazis—not only was he a non-German, he was Black!

While it was a blow to Nazi ideology that a Black man could out-perform his "Aryan" rivals, there was little that Hitler and his cohorts could do, other than vent their an-

FAST FACT

Jesse Owens was having difficulty with the trials for the long jump event at the Berlin Olympics. He had fouled on his first two jumps, and had only one more jump to go. If he fouled again, he would not advance to the finals. At that moment, in an unparalleled act of good sportsmanship, the German (and European) champion, **Carl Ludwig "Lutz" Long**, pointed out what Owens was doing wrong. Owens followed Long's advice, and not only did he qualify for the finals, he took the gold medal, placing ahead of Long, who took the silver. After the medal presentations,

noyance in private. Hitler came up with a fairly ingenious rationalization for Owens' superior performance. As he told his colleague Albert Speer, "people whose antecedents came from the jungle were primitive ... their physiques were stronger than those of civilized Whites." The solution to this dilemma?—in future, Blacks should be banned from sporting events such as the Olympics! To the author of *Mein Kampf* it all made perfect sense.

the two men walked to the dressing room, arm-in-arm, past Hitler and other Nazi dignitaries on the reviewing stand.

It was the beginning of a friendship that would last until 1943, when Long, a soldier in the German army, was killed in Italy. Long's last letter was to Owens and, fulfilling his last request, Owens served as best man at the wedding of Long's son Karl after the war.

"Lutz" Long was posthumously awarded the Pierre de Courbetin medal, given by the International Olympic Committee to athletes who demonstrate "the true spirit of sportsmanship" in Olympic events.

In the decades since the end of the Second World War and the defeat of Nazism, much has been made of the fact that Hitler refused to shake Jesse Owens' hand at the Olympic Games, but, in fairness, the whole story has seldom been told. On the first day of the Games, Hitler had shaken hands with each German medalist. At the end of the day, Olympic committee officials informed him that, as leader of the host nation, he should show impartiality: either he should greet every medal winner, regardless of nationality, or he should greet none at all. Hitler decided that he would henceforth congratulate none of them: thus, while it is true that he did not shake Owens' hand, neither did he shake hands with anyone else after that first day.

Jesse Owens himself stated that, as he passed the reviewing stand, Hitler rose and waved to him, a gesture which he returned. Although he had no use for Nazi theories of racial superiority, Owens maintained that he had not been ignored or avoided by Hitler. Rather, what truly wounded Owens occurred after he returned to the United States following his Olympic triumph. As he said himself, "Hitler didn't snub me—it was FDR [American President Franklin Delano Roosevelt] who snubbed me. The president didn't even send me a telegram."

A ticker-tape parade was organized for Owens in New York, followed by a reception at the Waldorf-Astoria Hotel in honour of his achievements. However, the reality of Owens' place in a racially divided United States was apparent even here. He had to take the hotel's freight elevator to the reception: only Whites were allowed to ride in the hotel's regular elevators.

Owens had hoped to take advantage of some of the lucrative contracts that awaited Olympic champions. However, because he was Black, none came his way, and he was forced to work as a gas station attendant. His athletic prowess became a caricature: in order to earn extra money for his family he would compete in races against dogs and horses. When asked why he degraded himself like this, Owens answered simply: "What was I supposed to do? I had four gold medals. But you can't eat four gold medals."

By the time Jesse Owens died in 1980, the American public had rediscovered him and his Olympic achievements. He was made a U.S. goodwill ambassador, and in 1990 he was posthumously awarded the Congressional Gold Medal.

THE BATTLE OF THE SEXES

For all of his life, Bobby Riggs had been very good at two things. The first was tennis: in both 1946 and 1947, Riggs was ranked as the No. 1 male tennis player in the world, The other thing at which Bobby excelled was self-promotion. As a matter of fact, by 1973 he was probably a better self-promoter than tennis player. But more on that in a moment.

After he had retired from the tennis circuit, Riggs had earned a small fortune as a hustler. Supremely confident, he generally bet on himself, and would lure his opponents in by agreeing to play with bizarre handicaps: for example, he played (and won!) one tennis match using a frying pan instead of a racquet. Bobby always did have one eye on the audience.

And so the decades passed—first the 1950s, then the 1960s. Then along came the 1970s. A new world was dawning, and Bobby needed a new angle. Playing tennis with a frying pan just didn't draw the crowds like it used to!

And then it came to him! The women's liberation movement was gaining steam in the early 1970s, and Bobby decided he would have none of it. After all, wasn't a woman's place in the home? So Bobby threw down the gauntlet: even though he was 55, and retired, he swore that he could still beat the best women players in the world. First he challenged Billie Jean King, who refused. Then, he challenged 30-year-old Margaret Court, the No. 1 seeded women's player of 1973, who accepted. To the consternation of women everywhere, Bobby actually won. Could it be true that men actually were better than women, as men had believed all along?? Bobbie got cocky. He taunted female tennis players everywhere, and the media picked up on the story. Bobby made the cover of both *Sports Illustrated* and *Time* magazine.

Enter 29-year-old Billie Jean King, that year's Wimbledon women's singles champion. Despite having earlier declined to play Riggs, she now felt that someone had to put him in his place—for the sake of women everywhere. The result was the "Battle of the Sexes," one of the most talked-about sporting events in history. It took place on September 20, 1973, in the Houston Astrodome, in front of a crowd in excess of 30,000 people. A further 50 million (!) watched the match on television. Bobby was back in the limelight, and loving it!

The pre-match festivities were much more about show business than about sport. Billie Jean entered the Astrodome first. Like Cleopatra, she was held aloft in a chair by four young musclemen, dressed like ancient slaves, their sweaty torsos gleaming in the lights. Not to be outdone, Bobby made his entrance in a rickshaw, pulled by a bevy of buxom young women whose costumes left little to the imagination. Bobby presented Billie Jean with an oversized lollypop—implying that she was a sucker to play him. Billie Jean presented Bobby with a piglet—implying that, in the feminist jargon of the day, he was a "male chauvinist pig." And then the best-of-five match began.

Tennis is about skill, but it is also about strategy and endurance. King had done her homework: she had analysed the match between Riggs and Court, and understood Riggs's style of play: finessing the ball, hitting gentle drop shots and soft lobs, and utilizing spin. Usually an aggressive player, Billie Jean decided she would have to beat Bobby at his own defensive game. She hugged the baseline, easily picking off his shots, but lobbing back hard, forcing Bobby to run from one end of the court to the other. Her strategy turned the "Battle of the Sexes" into the "Battle of the Generations," as Bobby's 55-year-old legs weren't up to the challenge. Puffing and thoroughly worn out, Bobby dropped three sets in a row: 6-4, 6-3 and 6-3. Not bad for an aging athlete, perhaps, but far short of his boast that he could beat any woman, any time. The "Battle of the Sexes" was over.

HAWK 'N' AWE

The relatively new sport of skateboarding seems to have gotten its start in California, sometime in the late 1940s or early 1950s. California, of course, is known for its summer days, sandy beaches, and tanned, sun-blond surfers—immortalized in such songs as "Surf City" by Jan and Dean, and "Surfin' Safari" by the Beach Boys. But what is less well known is that California's famous waves can sometimes be pretty flat, leaving shore-bound surfing enthusiasts with nothing but time on their hands. Bored silly, one—or maybe several—of these stranded surfers got the bright idea to nail some roller skating wheels onto the bottom of a board and *voila!*—the sport of skateboarding (originally known as "sidewalk surfing") was born.

The future of skateboarding would be forever altered on May 12, 1968. On that day, Frank and Nancy Hawk, of San Diego, California, became the proud parents of a bouncing bundle of joy: Anthony Frank Hawk, better known to his legion of fans as "Tony Hawk."

It appears that Tony was a hyperactive boy, and his older brother Steve, perhaps hoping to rid himself of a pesky little brother, bought 8-year-old Tony a used blue fibreglass banana board. The rest, as they say, is history. Tony's parents, relieved to have found an outlet for the boy's surplus energy, encouraged his interest in the sport. Frank even built a ramp (the first of many) for Tony in the backyard.

Tony was a natural. He practiced skateboarding for hours, seemingly impervious to skinned knees and bruised elbows. And he got better ... and better. So much better, in fact, that a mere six years later, at the tender age of 14, Tony turned pro. Tony's professional career would last for 17 years, during which time he became arguably the best skateboarder in the world. He participated in 103 professional events, winning 73 and placing second in 19 others.

Early on, Tony made a "wish list" of skateboard moves that he wanted to master. The list included moves with names such as the "ollie 540," the "kickflip 540," the "varial 720" and the all-but-impossible "900" (so called because it involves completing 2.5 revolutions—or 900 degrees—on the skateboard, while air-bound). Before Tony came along, no one had ever completed the "900." It was the Everest of skateboard manoeuvres. Indeed, some even whispered that it could never be done. But on July 27, 1999, Tony did it! It took him 11 attempts that day, but at age 31 Tony finally scaled his personal Everest. Having accomplished this amazing feat, Tony Hawk retired from professional skateboarding.

Hawk's retirement from the professional circuit marked the end of his competitive skating career, but it also marked the beginning of his legacy. In 1999, Hawk teamed with Activision and PlayStation® to launch a series of video games based on his skateboarding moves. To date, 15 titles have appeared and millions of copies have been sold; parents who check their children's collection of PlayStation® games are pretty much guaranteed to find one version or another of *Tony Hawk's Pro Skater*. In 2002 Tony launched the an-

FAST FACT

In 2006, Tony Hawk—along with other high-profile athletes such as André Agassi, Jeff Gordon, and Mario Lemieux—founded Athletes for Hope, an organization dedicated to helping athletes to get involved in philanthropy. Recognizing the power of sport to motivate people and to create bonds of friendship and goodwill, the founding athletes of Athletes for Hope wanted to establish a public charity that would inspire their fellow athletes, the entire sports industry, and the many fans of sport to commit time, energy and resources to make the world a better place.
www.athletesforhope.org

nual "Boom Boom Huck Jam," a 30-city arena tour that features "a mind-blowing two hours of music, mayhem and amazing skateboarding, BMX and motocross stunts."

Tony's post-retirement activities have made his name a household word and raised the profile and popularity of skateboarding to undreamed-of heights. No longer is the sport confined to sidewalks and empty swimming pools, or restricted to bored surfers and juvenile delinquents. Almost single-handedly, Tony Hawk pushed the sport of skateboarding from the fringe into the mainstream, making him one of the most celebrated and successful builders of sport in modern times.

PODIUM PROTEST

It was 1968. The Vietnam War was raging, and there was turmoil in the United States. The counter-culture was gaining momentum, and the Civil Rights movement was accelerating. Change and protest were in the air. It also happened to be the year of the XIX Summer Olympic Games, which were being held in Mexico City.

The Mexico City Games opened on October 12, and five days later, on October 17, the men's 200-metre race was run. The race was a close one. American sprinter Tommie Smith won the gold medal with a record-setting time of 19.83 seconds. Hot on Smith's heels was Australian Peter Norman, who posted a silver-medal time of 20.07 seconds, while American John Carlos finished a fractional .03 seconds behind Norman to take home the bronze with a time of 20.10 seconds. It was an impressive race, but not unlike hundreds that have been run at the Olympics, both before, and since. What was to make this race one for the books (including this book!) would take place during the medal presentation ceremony.

Both of the American medalists were Black, and they were proud to be Black. They were also members of the Olympic Project for Human Rights (OPHR), and were determined to seize the spotlight of their Olympic victory and use it to focus attention on the plight of their fellow Blacks who were suffering from the effects of racism and discrimination back in the United States.

On the way to the podium, Smith and Carlos told Peter Norman what they planned to do. Impressed, Norman immediately pledged his support and put his money where his mouth was, so to speak, by asking for an OPHR badge, which he then wore during the ceremony. The three men took their places on the presentation platform, the American and Australian flags were raised, and the band struck up "The Star-Spangled Banner."

As their national anthem played, Smith and Carlos bowed their heads, closed their eyes, and each man raised a single arm high into the air. Each man was wearing a black glove; each clenched his raised fist. Smith's raised right hand stood for the power of Black America, while Carlos's raised left hand stood for the unity of Black America. Neither man wore shoes, thus drawing attention to their black socks, which represented Black poverty in a racist America. They also wore black scarves, emphasizing Black pride. Carlos wore a string of beads that, in his words, "represented those individuals who were lynched, or killed and that no one said a prayer for, that were hung and tarred. It was for those thrown off the side of the boats in the 'middle passage' [the ocean voyage between Africa and North America during the slave trade]." At a press conference after the event, Smith stated: "If I win I am an American, not a Black American. But if I did something bad then they would say 'a Negro.' We are Black and we are proud of being Black ... Black America will understand what we did tonight." While their gesture remains one of the most powerful, non-violent racial protests in the history of sports, it was not without consequences.

Rule 51.3 of the Olympic Charter specifically states that "No kind of demonstration or political, religious, or racial propaganda is permitted at Olympic sites." As inspiring as it surely was to millions of Black Americans, there was no doubt that Smith's and Carlos' gesture was a political statement. As a result, both men were expelled from the Olympic Games, suspended from the U.S. team, and returned to the United States. Over the years that followed they received both praise and criticism for their gesture; they were also subjected to numerous death threats.

Ultimately, as times and attitudes changed, both men came to be seen as heroes of the Civil Rights movement. In 1984, Carlos would help to organize the Los Angeles Olympics, and in 1999 Smith received the Sportsman of the Millennium Award from the California Black Sports Hall of Fame.

But there was a third man on that podium, and the personal cost of Peter Norman's decision to stand in solidarity with his fellow medalists is often forgotten. Norman, who was White, was an opponent of Australia's racist "White only" immigration policy, which would not be repealed until 1973. As a result of his support for Smith and Carlos, which he demonstrated by wearing the OPHR badge, he was reprimanded by the Australian Olympic authorities, and banned from participating in the 1972 Olympic Games. Twenty-eight years later Norman's ostracism continued, and the Australian organizers for the 2000 Olympic Games held in Sydney, Australia, completed ignored him. He was not invited to the Games until members of the American delegation got wind of this shameful fact, and he attended as their guest.

Peter Norman died of a heart attack in Melbourne, Australia, on October 3, 2006. Both Tommie Smith and John Carlos gave eulogies and were pallbearers at his funeral.

9

E FOR EFFORT?

"WRONG WAY" RIEGELS

Roy Riegels is best remembered for his spectacular gaffe in the 1929 Rose Bowl. Riegels, a centre for the University of California, Berkeley, and an All-American to boot, gained a nickname—"Wrong Way"—and a place in football history, all because of a single misplayed fumble.

The University of California Golden Bears were grinding it out against the Georgia Tech Yellow Jackets into the second quarter, with the two sides deadlocked in a scoreless tie. Georgia Tech's J.C. "Stump" Thomason was running with the ball, but fumbled when he was hit by California's Benny Lom. Roy Riegels, Lom's defensive teammate, swooped in and picked up the football at the Georgia 30-yard-line and began his march to glory.

On his drive for the goal Riegels spun to avoid a hit. Then, to his surprise, he saw nothing but grass and daylight stretching ahead of him! Riegels began chugging toward the end zone, but all was not as it seemed for the excited young centre. In spinning away from the tackle, Riegels wound up facing in the wrong direction, and was now running towards his own end zone!

Benny Lom, meanwhile, was in hot pursuit, screaming at Riegels to stop. However, thinking that Lom just wanted the touchdown for himself, Riegels told him to back off. Seeing no other option, Lom desperately grabbed Roy and finally stopped him on the California three-yard line. Turning "Wrong Way" back the *right way*, Lom explained what

FAST FACT

One athlete who can perhaps relate to Roy Riegels is Steve Smith (now retired), who played for the Edmonton Oilers of the National Hockey League. It was April 23, 1986, and defenseman Steve Smith was feeling lucky. It was his 23rd birthday, and he just had a feeling he was going to score. It was game 7 of the playoff series between the Edmonton Oilers and their provincial rivals, the Calgary Flames. The score was tied 2-2, with 5:28 remaining in the third period.

had happened: Riegels had sprinted 62 yards in the wrong direction! By the time he was turned around and ready to go back the other way, however, he faced a wall of Georgia Tech players. The ensuing tackle smashed Riegels back to his one-yard line.

California tried to punt the ball away to mitigate the damage, but the kick was blocked, resulting in the Golden Bears spotting the Yellow Jackets a safety and a 2-0 lead.

Mortified, Reigels wanted to sit out the rest of the game, but California coach Clarence "Nibs" Price convinced him

The Oilers' goalie, Grant Fuhr, passed the puck to Smith, behind the net, so that it could be cleared out of the Oilers' zone. Not missing a beat, Smith slapped the puck. Unfortunately, instead of sailing down the ice, the puck bounced off Fuhr and back into the Oilers' net! Steve Smith had indeed scored— and he'd scored the game-winning, series-winning goal, no less—but he'd scored into his own net!

That goal haunted Smith for the rest of his career as an Oiler, for every time his team played in Calgary, and Smith touched the puck, the entire Calgary crowd would yell "SHOOT!"

to go back in and Reigels played a strong second half. However, as both teams went on to score only one touchdown apiece, the safety held up as the difference, crowning Georgia Tech as the 1929 Rose Bowl champs over the beleaguered California squad by a final score of 8-7.

Riegels atoned for his mistake by putting together a great All-American season the next year, but from that day forward, he was forever known as "Wrong Way" Riegels. He went on to appear on television a few times because of the misdirected "touchdown" dash, and in 1991 he was inducted into the Rose Bowl Hall of Fame.

THE "ROCKET" RICHARD RIOT

Maurice "Rocket" Richard, who grew up in the tough Bordeaux area of Montreal, was one of hockey's most prolific goal scorers, becoming the first player to reach 50 goals—which he did in 50 games—and the first to reach 500 career points. Richard was held in such high regard by the home-town fans of the Montreal Canadiens ("the Habs") that his suspension actually provoked a riot: the infamous "Richard Riot" of March 17, 1955.

The 1954–55 NHL season was drawing to a close, and the Montreal Canadiens' biggest star, the "Rocket," appeared destined to win his first NHL scoring title. That dream, however, came to an abrupt end on March 13 as Richard momentarily "lost it." It all began when a high stick from Boston Bruin Hal Laycoe resulted in a bloody gash on Richard's forehead. Richard went after Laycoe who, having already dropped his gloves and stick, was ready and waiting. Or so he thought. Richard obviously had other plans as he laid some lumber of his own. He not only attacked Laycoe with his stick, but also punched linesman Cliff Thompson, who was attempting to restrain the "Rocket." When the dust had settled, Richard stood there with an unconscious linesman at his feet.

As a result of Richard's wild actions (and because this was the second incident of the season in which Richard had assaulted an official), NHL president Clarence Campbell suspended him for the rest of the season, including the playoffs. The suspension, although warranted, came at the most inopportune time for both the Canadiens and Richard, as the Canadiens were fighting for first place with the Detroit Red Wings.

The Habs' next home game was against the Red Wings, and in attendance was none other than Clarence Campbell. The air was thick with tension and when Campbell arrived, the fans were so livid that they proceeded to pelt him with eggs and other debris, and continued doing so each time the Wings scored. Allegedly, one fan even walked up to Campbell and offered him a handshake, but instead gave the president an open-hand slap on the face. Campbell remained seated through much of the abuse until a fan set off a tear gas bomb, at which point the Forum had to be evacuated and the game was forfeited to the Red Wings.

The livid mob of Quebeckers wasn't finished just yet, though, as they took the riot outside the Forum. Nothing was safe for blocks on every side, as hundreds of stores were looted and vandalized, and approximately $500,000 damage was done to the Forum itself. The riot finally came to an end at 3 a.m., with 25 police officers and civilians injured, and scores of rioters arrested.

Now sidelined, the "Rocket" would lose the scoring title—in the last game of the season—to teammate Bernard "Boom Boom" Geoffrion, who was actually booed by his own team's fans! The Canadiens would also lose the Stanley Cup in seven games to none other than the Detroit Red Wings.

Even though his suspension might have cost the Canadiens the Cup that season, Richard went on to lead his teammates to five consecutive Stanley Cup wins in the following years—a record that stands to this day.

THE WORST
APPROACH

The 1999 British Open had many golfing superstars contending for the prestigious major championship. Names like Justin Leonard, Angel Cabrera, Tiger Woods, Greg Norman, Reteif Goosen, and Jim Furyk highlighted the field. However, it was a little-known Frenchman named Jean Van de Velde who was leading the pack. Van de Velde had played brilliantly throughout the tournament. As he came to the final hole, a hole which he had birdied in each of his last two rounds, he was enjoying a comfortable three-stroke lead.

As the confident Frenchman teed up his aggressive final drive, his victory appeared to be so certain that the engravers had already begun placing his name on the trophy. After all, Van de Velde needed to score no worse than a six on the par-4 72nd hole to win. A mere double bogey would suffice.

As commentators and fans watched Van de Velde taking practice swings, something seemed amiss—and it seemed to be his decision-making process. Van de Velde was warming up with his driver when a water hazard lay in front of him. Laying up with an iron would have been the appropriate choice. But he swung away anyhow.

His drive stayed dry, coming to a halt yards before the water hazard but past the fairway and lying in the rough. Not a travesty. He was still safe and had a playable lie. But instead of taking the logical route and playing an easy shot back to the fairway ahead, leaving a short chip and two putts for the win, Van de Velde chose to take an aggressive line at the hole down the hazard-strewn right side.

Van de Velde dug in and smacked the ball, which took an unfavourable bounce and settled into the long, thick rough. The sensible play here would have been to play a shot back toward the fairway for a simple chip onto the green and one putt to victory. But, now seemingly resolved to blow a major championship, Van de Velde decided to attack the green over another water hazard!

His third shot struggled to fight out of the thick rough to become airborne, which it did, albeit for a short journey into the creek. Van de Velde, evidently feeling that victory was still within his grasp, started removing his shoes and socks and rolling up his pant legs. Yes—he had decided to play the ball out of the water hazard and save the stroke he would have been penalized for having to drop the ball! He scaled down the short wall into the creek and stared down at his ball before suddenly snapping back to reality. He realized in that cold, lonely moment in the creek that he was about to try to shoot a ball out of the water, a nearly impossible shot. Back to his senses, and trying to revive his rapidly fading dream, Van de Velde opted to drop his ball and take a penalty stroke, leaving him the chance to chip on and putt in to salvage a victory. He then dropped his ball into the thick rough—he had no other option—and settled into position, apparently thinking clearly for the first time in 15 minutes.

Unfortunately for Van de Velde, he flubbed his fifth shot into the greenside bunker and it seemed as if all was lost. Now he would have to chip in from the sand to win.

His playing partner, Australian Craig Parry, had been watching events unfold. Like Van de Velde, his ball rested in the greenside bunker. All Van de Velde had to do was sink the same shot his partner had just made. So with the crowd sympathetically cheering him on, Van de Velde made one final attempt to seal the British Open victory. He smoothly swung his club and contacted the ball, sending it cleanly into the air toward the hole. His ball rolled steadily across the green and ... ended up 2 metres (6 feet) left of the hole.

Now he had to sink this putt just to tie and force a playoff with Justin Leonard and Paul Lawrie. Van de Velde strode up to the ball and authoritatively drained it into the heart of the cup. There was still a chance. Unfortunately, Van de Velde's inept play continued in the playoff holes and he was never a threat. Paul Lawrie won the 1999 British Open.

Tournament officials raced to get Van de Velde's name off the trophy and replace it with that of the winner. The engraving task was completed just in time for Lawrie to raise the trophy.

Van de Velde and his supporters were in shock over the catastrophe. For 15 long, incomprehensible minutes, he had clearly taken the worst approach to each play, costing him the tournament. To this day, the blunder remains Jean Van de Velde's greatest claim to fame. His crumbling on July 18, 1999, at the British Open lives in infamy as one of the worst collapses in sporting history.

10

TRIUMPH OVER TRAGEDY

HOTTER
THAN A PISTOL

Much of the sports world is focused on professional teams, elite athletes, and world-record performances. But sports touches and enriches the lives of ordinary people, too, and every once in a while, a story comes along that reminds us of the true meaning of sports, and the important role it can play in the lives of young people. This is one of those stories.

When he was two years old, Jason McElwain of Greece, New York, was diagnosed with autism—a neural disorder that can affect social interaction and communication. But Jason—"J-Mac" to his friends—refused to consider his condition as a handicap: in his own words, it was "not a big deal." He was just like everyone else.

Like so many teenagers, J-Mac loved sports. As his father David said, sports were "his equalizer." And like so many teenagers, J-Mac had a dream. It was a modest dream by some standards, but to J-Mac, it was important. Of all sports, J-Mac loved basketball the most, and more than anything else, he wanted to play on his high school basketball team, the Greece Athena Trojans. But J-Mac was only 5'6" tall, too short to make the roster.

Instead of being angry or disappointed, J-Mac decided to sign on as the Trojans' team manager, and for the next three years, during basketball season he was behind the bench. With his white shirt and black tie, he became a team fixture, handing out sweat towels, filling water bottles, encouraging the players—in short, doing whatever he could to help the team. In those three years, he missed only one game, and the Trojans, and his fellow students, appreciated his efforts. They loved the little guy. But deep down, J-Mac still dreamed of making the team and getting the chance to play the game he loved.

On February 15, 2006, J-Mac got his shot. It was the last home game of the season, and J-Mac would be graduating that spring. It was now or never, and team coach Jim Johnson decided to recognize J-Mac's hard work for the team. That night, instead of cheering from the sidelines, J-Mac would be suited up and on the bench. There were no guarantees that he would get to play, but for that one night, he would really, truly be part of the team. J-Mac was a Trojan!

J-Mac's story could have ended there, but it didn't. With about four minutes left in the game, the Trojans had a healthy lead, and Coach Johnson gave J-Mac the nod. The excited

17-year-old practically flew onto the court, and the crowd went wild, cheering on their friend!

The Trojans got possession of the ball and marched down the court. J-Mac was in position on the right side baseline, and with 3:46 left in the game, the ball came to him. J-Mac took the shot from the three-point line ... and missed. It was an air ball (basketball jargon for a shot that misses the basket completely, failing to hit the rim, backboard or even the net). Oh well!

And then, something truly magical happened. Thirty-four seconds later, the ball came to J-Mac again. From the three-point baseline he set his stance and took the shot. This time,

FAST FACT

Since his amazing performance, Jason McElwain has met President George W. Bush and Magic Johnson, has won the ESPY award for the best moment in sports in 2006—beating out Kobe Bryant's 81-point game!—and has appeared on *Oprah, Good Morning America, SportsCenter, CNN,* and *Today.* He has his own Topps trading card and has appeared in a Gatorade commercial.

it went in! But the game wasn't finished yet, and neither was J-Mac: the ball kept coming to him and he kept hitting shot after shot after shot. It seemed he *couldn't* miss. In his own words, "The basket was like this great big old huge bucket. It was huge." Six three-pointers in a row! And then, with three seconds left, halfway between centre court and the three-point line J-Mac threw up a Hail Mary. The ball sailed in the air towards the hoop, but did it have the line? Did it even have the legs? Of course it did! What would a Cinderella story be without a buzzer-beater? J-Mac nailed it in the heart of the hoop to go out on the highest high of his life. When asked about the experience afterwards, J-Mac, who was the game's top scorer and now holds the school record of 20 points in less than four minutes, said, "I was on fire. I was hotter than a pistol."

Sometimes, hoop dreams do come true.

BROTHERS
IN ARMS

On December 8, 2001, Leroy Sutton regained consciousness and pulled back the covers of his hospital bed. He remembered being struck by the train, but nothing prepared him for what he saw: both of his legs were gone.

Such a loss might have been overwhelming, but not so for Leroy. Determined that he would not be bound to a wheelchair for the rest of his life, the 11-year-old undertook a vigorous weight-lifting routine to increase his upper body strength, so that he could move around freely with just his arms. So strong did Leroy become that, by his freshman year, a friend suggested he consider trying out for the high school wrestling team.

Leroy did just that, and furthermore, he made the team. While many people might have thought it impossible for someone with no legs to succeed as a wrestler, Leroy—through a combination of courage, determination, and sheer physical strength—beat the odds. Not only was he a wrestler, but he was a good one, winning the majority of his hard-fought matches.

In 2008, Leroy transferred to Lincoln-West High School in Cleveland, Ohio, for his senior year. He immediately signed up for the wrestling team, and there he met a fellow wrestler who was his match in terms of strength, courage and determination.

Dartanyon Crockett was born with Leber's disease, a condition that results in an acute loss of central vision. Dartanyon is legally blind, barely making out the facial features of individuals sitting right beside him, and seeing only rough shapes passing or coming towards him. Like Leroy, however, Dartanyon refused to allow his disability to get the better of him, and, like Leroy, he found wrestling to be a sport that allowed him to compete on an equal basis with other students.

In fact, as astonishing as it sounds, Dartanyon was more than the equal of his peers: he dominated the other wrestlers against whom he competed. In his last year of high school, Dartanyon had a record of 26 victories and only 3 losses, and he won the league championship in his weight class.

Leroy and Dartanyon met on the wrestling mat and formed an instant bond. Both were phenomenally strong, near equals in physical strength. Both could be construed as "handicapped," although it was a term that both rejected: in fact, as far as their wrestling was concerned, each was able to turn his "handicap" into an asset when competing against "normal" wrestlers.

Leroy and Dartanyon's sparring partnership quickly developed into a deep friendship. Although neither young man could remember when it first started, Dartanyon began carrying Leroy on his back in those places that did not have wheelchair access, and onto and off school buses. Dartanyon summarized their relationship: "I'm his wheelchair. He's also my drill partner and teammate, and I'd carry him to his next match at another school if no bus were available." Nor was the relationship one-sided. Rather, Leroy would direct the nearly sightless Dartanyon as they navigated their way down stairways and hallways. If Dartanyon was Leroy's wheelchair, Leroy was Dartanyon's eyes. And every time that his friend would wrestle, Leroy would sit by the edge of the mat, coaching and encouraging him, observing how he could improve his "game." As Dartanyon said, "It's like having my brother there." Together, as a team, they were stronger than either was as an individual.

They helped each other emotionally, as well, able to joke about their disabilities in a way that their other friends could not. Dartanyon could remind Leroy, "Don't forget your shoes..." and Leroy could reply, "You just can't see them." It helped to relieve the sting of being different. The boys were a perfect fit. They joked together, they travelled together, they wrestled together, and most importantly, together they conquered the challenges that they faced.

At the end of the school year, Leroy and Dartanyon overcame another obstacle. Both boys beat the odds and graduated—an accomplishment that eluded a majority of Lincoln-West's students. On graduation night, they made their way across the stage to receive their diplomas. This time, however, there was a difference. Leroy had just been fitted with a set of prosthetic legs, and instead of depending on Dartanyon to carry him, Leroy asked his friend to walk beside him. "It was a privilege, it was an honour, to be the one to walk with him," Dartanyon said. "There's nothing this man sitting right next to me can't do, and he's proven that time and time again." Leroy replied: "It meant so much to me to know, I have a friend that was there to catch me when I was stumbling."

THE MARATHON OF HOPE

Some of us run for sport, some of us run for lifestyle, and some of us run for fun. But Terry Fox ran for hope. The iconic image of the 21-year-old, curly-haired amputee running along the side of the road, escorted by police cars, will be forever etched in the minds of Canadians, and stands as one of the most inspiring stories of youthful courage of all time.

Terry was born on July 28, 1958, in Winnipeg, Manitoba, but moved with his family to British Columbia when he was 8 years old. He loved sports, and made up in determination what he lacked in size, practicing for hours in the evenings and on weekends to improve his skills. By the time he graduated, Terry was voted co-athlete of the year for his high school. His interest in sports and fitness led Terry to register in the kinesiology program at Simon Fraser University, with a goal of eventually becoming a high school physical education teacher. That dream would be cut short in the most tragic way.

In November 1977, persistent pain in his knee forced Terry to visit the doctor. The news he received was horrifying for the 19-year-old athlete: he was diagnosed with osteosarcoma, a malignant bone cancer that is prevalent in tubular long bones. Doctors told him that his only chance for survival would involve the amputation of his right leg, 15 cm (6 inches) above his knee.

Rather than retreating into bitterness and despair, Terry responded with gritty determination. Within six months of the surgery he was playing golf, having been fitted with a prosthetic leg. He also went through 16 months of chemotherapy, during which many of his fellow patients did not survive. Their suffering inspired Terry, but what could he do to help? Then, the idea came to him: he, an amputee, would run across Canada, raising funds for cancer research. His goal was to raise $24 million—a dollar for every man, woman, and child in Canada.

Terry's goal would not be an easy undertaking: Canada is the second largest country on earth, stretching some 5,000 miles (8,000 kilometres) from coast to coast. Indeed, given the rigours of the Canadian landscape, many believed that the task was impossible. Undaunted, Terry began his "Marathon of Hope" on April 12, 1980, by dipping his prosthetic leg into the icy waters of the Atlantic Ocean off of St. John's, Newfoundland. He filled two water bottles—one for himself, as a souvenir, the other to be poured into the Pacific Ocean at the end of his journey. He was 21 years old.

At first, few Canadians knew of Fox's mission. However, as he persevered through the Maritime provinces, local news stations began to carry his story, and the national media began to take notice. As spring turned to summer, Terry continued to run an average of 26 miles (42 km) per day: the equivalent of running a full-length marathon every single day. Through wind and rain, heat and cold, up hills and down, he ran. He ran through towns in the Maritimes, Quebec, and then Ontario, greeted by cheering citizens who made donations to his cause, and ever-increasing media attention. Police cruisers, lights flashing, accompanied him through high-traffic areas. The Canadian Cancer Society arranged for him to address a variety of events. He met the Prime Minister and Governor-General, as well as countless athletes, local dignitaries, and average citizens. Terry's profile grew, and enthusiasm for his cause gained momentum. By the time he reached Thunder Bay, Ontario, he had raised $1.7 million for cancer research.

At Thunder Bay, Terry's personal marathon ended. Experiencing ever-greater fatigue and a painful cough, he finally sought medical advice. The news was of the worst possible sort: his cancer had returned and his condition was terminal. He had run for 143 days, covering an amazing 3,339 miles (5,373 km).

On September 2, Terry Fox held a tearful press conference during which he announced that his cancer had returned and spread to his lungs. Thousands of Canadians watched the broadcast and wept with him, and the nation rose to meet the challenge Terry had set before it. A week after his run ended, a nation-wide telethon raised over $10 million for the Marathon of Hope, and by the following spring, Terry's original goal of $24 million had been surpassed.

Like Pheidippides, the original Marathon runner, Terry Fox carried a message of hope. And, like Pheidippides, he did not live long enough to see the fruits of his personal marathon. Terry Fox died on June 28, 1981—one month before his 22nd birthday.

Terry Fox is commemorated across Canada: streets, roads, schools and even a mountain bear his name. His statue can

FAST FACT

When Terry Fox died, then Prime Minister Pierre E. Trudeau ordered flags across the country to be flown at half-mast: a rare honour usually reserved for statesmen. The Prime Minister addressed the House of Commons, stating: "It occurs very rarely in the life of a nation that the courageous spirit of one person unites all people in the celebration of his life and in the mourning of his death... We do not think of him as one who was defeated by misfortune but as one who inspired us with the example of the triumph of the human spirit over adversity."

be found in several cities, and the government of Canada issued a commemorative stamp honouring Terry shortly after his death. However, perhaps the greatest and most enduring testament to Terry's Marathon of Hope is to be found in the thousands of Canadians who have been cured of cancer because of his run—many of whom were not even born when Terry began the final stage of his life's journey. In the 30 years since Terry's death, more than $400 million has been raised for cancer research through Canada's annual Terry Fox Run.

11

APPARITIONS AND SUPERSTITIONS

OBSESSIVE COMPULSIVE ORDER

With non-stop pressure to perform, and to be a role model besides, it's no wonder certain athletes sometimes seem a little crazy. However, there might actually be some method to their madness! Social theorists such as Graham I. Neil note that, despite all of an athlete's planning, scouting, research, and training, there is still an element of chance in every competition. And it turns out that superstition is a common coping mechanism for dealing with "chance." Superstition allows an athlete to remain psychologically stable by creating the façade that everything, including chance, is accounted for. Thus, athletes are basically "self-medicating," and superstition is their prescription drug of choice! It should also be noted that some sports psychologists have even drawn parallels between spirituality and superstition as a trigger for the release of various performance-enhancing neurochemicals. So it is possible that athletes' superstitions are indeed justified and have an actual physiological bearing on performance!

With this in mind, here are a few of some of the more outlandish (and entertaining) superstitions from professional sports:

- For 11 years of his playing career, MLB pitcher Turk Wendell was known as much for his peculiar superstitions as he was for his fastball or changeup. Apparently, Wendell had an obsession with hygiene. During every inning, he would be sure to chew four sticks of licorice while he pitched. When the inning

FAST FACT

Some sports psychologists, drawing on the research of Swiss neurologist Peter Brugger and NIH geneticist Dean Hamer, believe that there may be a connection between the VMAT2 gene, which is associated with spirituality, and the human body's main performance-enhancing chemicals: norepeinephrine (a chemical that activates the body's fight or flight response, triggers the release of glucose from energy stores, and increases blood flow to skeletal muscle) and dopamine

ended, like clockwork he would sprint back to the dugout, jump over the baseline like a kindergarten student on a walk, and then proceed to brush his teeth while his team was at bat. After 11 years, that's a lot of scrubbing on the pearly whites.

- Before Jason Terry broke into the NBA with the Atlanta Hawks, in college he started the ritual of sleeping in his uniform the night before each game. He believed that this would get him in the proper frame of mind and make it feel like the game started sooner. When the young three-point-shooting speedster

(a chemical which can increase blood pressure, heart rate, and produce the sensation of pleasure that accompanies the accomplishment of a goal). What they found was that those with a specific variation of the VMAT2 gene that increases the brain's production of these chemicals are also the individuals who score highest on psychological tests for spirituality. Since these neurochemicals are associated with spirituality and superstition as well as athletic performance, there could be a connection between superstition and increased athletic performance.

joined the NBA, he went a step farther and started wearing the team shorts of his next opponent to bed. Which meant that Terry had to own game shorts for all 30 NBA teams, and a really big suitcase if he was going on a long road trip!

- After a lengthy "point-less" streak in his rookie season with the Ottawa Senators, Bruce Gardiner decided to go to teammate Tom Chorske for advice. Chorske told him he was being too nice to his stick, and needed to teach his twig to show him a little more respect by dunking it in the toilet! After a little hesitation, and a few more "point-less" games, Gardiner acquiesced and gave his blade the recommended toilet swirley. The next game the rookie broke out of his slump and went on a tear. After that, he used this unconventional method as a slump-ender whenever needed.

- Cleveland Indians outfielder Kevin Rhomberg played 41 games in the "Bigs," but the most lasting impression he left was his superstitions. If anyone touched Rhomberg at any time, he would have to touch that individual back. He didn't even try to hide it. If he was tagged out on the base paths, he would wait until the end of the inning, search out the player who had tagged him, and run over and tag him back! On top of that, Rhomberg refused to make right turns on the field. If necessary, he would make a left circle rather than take the short right-turn route.

- Sidney Crosby will not let anybody touch his hockey stick after he has taped it. If someone does touch it, he peels off the tape and tapes the stick again.

- MLB star Wade Boggs would eat chicken before every game, take exactly 150 ground balls in warm ups, hit the batting cages at exactly 5:17 p.m. and do his wind sprints at exactly 7:17 p.m. before evening games, and write the word "chai"—a Hebrew word meaning "life"—in the dirt before every at-bat.

- Before every game, Indianapolis Colts quarter-back Peyton Manning reads the game program cover-to-cover.

THE CURSE OF
THE BAMBINO?

He was "the Wali of Wallop," the "Behemoth of Bust," the "Colossus of Clout," the "King of Crash," the "Titan of Terror," the "Sultan of Swat," the "Great Bambino." He was, of course, the one and only Babe Ruth—one of the greatest sports heroes in American culture. However, Ruth is remembered not only for his legendary on-field achievements. It has also been alleged that the Bambino was behind the 86-year World Series drought of the Boston Red Sox: the so-called "Curse of the Bambino."

Until 1918, the Red Sox were the most successful club in major league baseball, having captured five World Series championships in the leagues' first 15 years. One of the rising stars of the Boston team was a promising young pitcher and slugger named George Herman Ruth. Ruth was a phenomenal pitcher with the Sox, going 89-46 with a career ERA of only 2.28, and he was the lead pitcher for the Sox in their 1916 and 1918 World Series triumphs. At the same time, he was also blossoming into quite the slugger, batting .289 with 49 home runs in 391 at-bats. Obviously, the Babe was a valuable member of the Boston franchise, and fans anticipated many more championship seasons to come.

Then, the unthinkable happened. In the 1919–20 off-season, Boston owner Harry Frazee, frustrated with Ruth's demands for a raise, sold him to the lowly New York Yankees for $100,000, and a $300,000 loan.

Until the trade, the Yankees had been floundering, and had never won a championship title. But all of that would now change. On May 1, 1920, Ruth scored his first home run as a Yankee against ... the Boston Red Sox. In 1921, the Yankees won their first of 40 American League pennants. Two years later, in 1923, they went even further, winning their first of 27 World Series victories. In all, Ruth would play on seven pennant- and four World Series–winning teams during his years with the Yankees. Even more humiliating for Boston, in ten of the next twelve seasons following "the trade," the Babe would out-homer the entire Boston team. And if the "Bambino" trade had reversed the fortunes of the New York Yankees, it seemed also to have sent the Red Sox into a tailspin, for it would be 86 long years before Boston would again take home baseball's biggest prize!

As decade after decade went by, Boston fans were left scratching their heads. What had gone wrong? What had happened to the team's glory days? It would be more than a quarter of a century, in 1946, before the Sox made their next World Series appearance, losing to the St. Louis Cardinals in seven. Between 1946 and 2004, the team would reach the finals a further three times, losing each series in the seventh game. There were whispers of a curse.

In 1949, the Red Sox needed just one more victory to clinch the AL pennant. They lost the last two games of the season to ... the Yankees! Adding insult to injury, the Yankees would go on that year to win the first of a record five straight World Series. There were other memorable losses. In 1978, the Sox were leading the Yankees by 14 games in the AL East Division pennant race. Then, the Sox slumped and the Yankees surged, culminating in a four-game sweep known to Red Sox fans as the "Boston Massacre," in which the Yankees outscored the Sox 42-9. Tied for the lead with the Yankees at the end of the season, the Sox would then lose a heartbreaker: a one-game playoff for the title. The Yankees again went on to take the World Series. The whispers of a curse turned into mumbles.

In 1986, the mumbles of a curse turned into a roar. The Sox were leading another New York team—this time, the Mets—by three games to two in the World Series, and were up 5-3 as they went to the bottom of the 10th. Boston's relief pitcher, Calvin Schiraldi, struck out the first two Mets at bat. The end of the drought was in sight! Only one more "out" and the Series was theirs. But it was not to be. The Mets scored three unanswered runs and won the game 6-5. Two days later, the Sox would lose the seventh and deciding game 8-5, after at one point leading 3-0. It couldn't have happened... but it did.

So, the Red Sox indeed seemed to be cursed. But what was behind the curse? Theories abounded, but then, in 1990, Dan Shaughnessy, a writer for the *Boston Globe*, seemed to hit upon the perfect reason for the Red Sox' woes and the Yankees' wins. It was the Bambino. That infamous trade! In his book, *The Curse of the Bambino*, Shaughnessy identified the 1919–20 trade as the turning point in the fortunes of both the Red Sox and the Yankees. His theory caught on, and for the next 14 years, whenever the Sox played in Yankee Stadium, the crowd would roar "1918!"—the last time the Sox had taken the World Series.

Was there really a curse? If so, would it end? And, most important to Red Sox fans, if the curse was going to end, when would it be?

THE CURSE
REVERSED

The year: 1992. The place: Boston's Fenway Park. In an effort to reverse the now-legendary "Curse of the Bambino," frustrated fans enlisted Father Guido Sarducci, of *Saturday Night Live* fame, to perform an exorcism. It would be another losing season for the Sox, who finished in seventh place in the AL East, with a record of 73 wins and 89 losses. Maybe the fans should have brought in a real priest?

The year: 1994. The place: a television studio. During the filming of Ken Burns' documentary entitled *Baseball*, Bill Lee, a former Red Sox pitcher, suggested, tongue-in-cheek, that the Sox should exhume Babe Ruth's body, transport it to Fenway Park, and officially apologize for the 1919–20 trade. Of course, the Babe's body remains undisturbed at the Cemetery of the Gate of Heaven in Hawthorne, New York. But the 1994 playing season was cut short by a players strike that year, and the World Series was cancelled. The Sox had finished fourth in the AL East, with a record of 54 wins and 61 losses. Perhaps Bill Lee's suggestion should have been taken seriously.

The year: 1999. The place: Fenway Park. The Red Sox, playing against none other than the New York Yankees in the AL East Division championships, bring in Julia Ruth Stevens, the Babe's daughter, to throw the first pitch of Game 4. This attempt to assuage the shade of the Bambino met with no success. The Yankees took the series in five games. What would have happened if she had thrown the first pitch in the series opener, instead?

The year: 2001. The place: the top of the world. In his effort to "reverse the curse," Boston Red Sox fan Paul Giorgio climbed Mt. Everest, and left a Sox cap at the summit. For extra measure, he burned a Yankee cap at the base camp. That season, the Sox finished second in the AL East division, with 82 wins and 79 losses. Maybe Giorgio should have burned an entire Yankee uniform.

The year: 2002. The place: Wallis Pond, Sudbury, Massachusetts. Legend had it that the Bambino had tossed his piano into the pond when he lived in Sudbury. Hoping to mollify his ghost, fans attempted to find and raise the piano. They didn't. That year, the Sox again finished second in the AL East, with 93 wins and 69 losses. But at least their record was improving.

The year: Unknown. The place: Storrow Drive, Boston. An anonymous fan paints over the "Reverse Curve" sign to read "Reverse the Curse." For years, the sign was cleaned, only to have the message reappear. Was this a silent plea to the baseball gods? The graffiti only disappeared for good after 2004—to which we now turn.

The year: 2004. The place: Boston's Fenway Park. It was Game 4 of the American League Championship Series. The Boston Red Sox were down three games to none, the Yankees were up 4-3 in the bottom of the ninth, and it seemed as though the shade of Babe Ruth was once again haunting the Red Sox and their fans. But, with a walk, a stolen base, and an RBI single off legendary closer Mariano Rivera, the Sox tied the game and sent it into extra frames. The game went on for three more innings until David "Big Papi" Ortiz

FAST FACT

So why was the curse reversed in 2004? The writers at *Saturday Night Live* had a theory, which they wrote into the "Weekend Update." In the skit, the Bambino's ghost confesses that, during Game Four, he thought the Yankees had the series in the bag. Confident that his curse was still working, he left the game to go out drinking with the ghosts of Mickey Mantle and Rodney Dangerfield ... and the rest is history.

made a two-run hit in the bottom of the twelfth to send Red Sox fans into a frenzy. The Sox went on to win the next three games, becoming the first team in major league baseball history to win a seven-game series after being down three games. The Sox then swept the St. Louis Cardinals in four games, and at last laid to rest the tired old Bronx cheer, "1918!" The "Curse of the Bambino" was broken!

THE SALT LAKE LOONIE

The value of the Canadian dollar has had its ups and downs over the years, but one Canadian dollar in particular—the Salt Lake Loonie—will always be worth its weight in gold to Canadians.

The legend of the Salt Lake Loonie began at the centre ice line of the E-Center in Salt Lake City, Nevada, during the 2002 Winter Olympics, where a Canadian by the name of Trent Evans was helping to install the ice for the Games. Although Canadians pride themselves on having the best hockey players in the world, at the time of the Salt Lake City Olympics, Canada had not won an Olympic Men's Hockey gold medal since 1952, and had never won gold in Women's Hockey. As he helped to prepare the Olympic ice, expert ice maker Trent Evans found himself with an opportunity to bring a little extra luck to his northern compatriots, perhaps just enough luck to break their 50-year gold-medal drought.

National Hockey League rinks have a clearly marked centre, which the ice-makers use as a crucial point of reference in laying out the lines and faceoff circles, especially the 12-inch, blue centre-ice faceoff circle that assists with the puck drop. When Trent Evans arrived at the Salt Lake City E Center, he found no such centre marker, and he and the other ice makers worked hard to be sure that the lines of play and faceoff circles, as well as the Olympic logos, would be correctly aligned and placed. At last, they had it all right, but Evans still had no marker to indicate the centre puck-drop location. He consulted with one of his fellow Canadian ice-makers, who knew that at the Olympic practice rinks a splotch of yellow paint had been used. *How big?* Evans asked. *About the size of a loonie* was the reply.

Initially, Evans marked the spot with the only thing he had handy—a Canadian dime—intending to come back later with the yellow paint. But that night, he had a idea: instead of a splotch of yellow paint the size of a loonie, perhaps a *real loonie* marking centre ice would bring the Canadian teams a little bit of extra luck. Before the final floodings, Evans chipped away the ice above his already buried dime, and placed a loonie over it.

Obscured by the ice, the loonie probably would never have been noticed, save for the fact that Evans told his secret to at least one too many people: the organizing committee caught wind of Evans' clever ploy and ordered that the loonie be removed. Instead of replacing the loonie with a splotch of yellow paint, Evans simply used the yellow paint to *hide* his lucky loonie. Problem solved.

The stage was now set for one of the most memorable hockey tournaments in Olympic history. Both the men's and women's gold medal matches would be an entirely North American affair, north versus south, Canada versus the United States. Interest on both sides of the 49th parallel was high, and so were tensions.

First up was the women's final on February 21, 2002. The Canadian women, who had gone undefeated in the round robin with 25 goals for and 0 goals against, were the heavy favourites. Although they had been pencilled in to walk away with the gold, in the end, they only narrowly defeated the United States, with a 3-2 victory. Three days later, on February 24, 2002, fifty years to the day since Canada's last Olympic gold in men's hockey, the Canadian men's team skated onto the ice of the E-Center. The rest, as they say, is history: Canada took the gold medal game 5-2.

After the game, Evans chipped the "Salt Lake Loonie" out of the ice and presented it to Wayne Gretzky, who was the executive director of the men's hockey team. Gretzky would later present the lucky coin to the Hockey Hall of Fame in Toronto, where it was officially inducted on March 8, 2002—an odd inductee in the view of non-Canadians, perhaps, but an entirely fitting one in a nation that is absolutely fanatical about its hard-hitting, fast-paced, rock 'em–sock 'em national sport.

About the Illustrator

wight Allott graduated from the Alberta College of Art and Design in 1984. Over the course of his career, he has earned awards in *Applied Arts* and *Communication Arts*. His work has appeared in the *Wall Street Journal*, *Sports Illustrated*, and even on a billboard in Times Square.

About the Authors

Brett and Jesse Matlock were born and raised in small-town Saskatchewan. Growing up in a sports-centric family pushed both Brett and Jesse to a love of sport. The brothers Matlock have well-rounded sports pedigrees. With degrees in Sociology and Anthropology from the University of Regina, both Brett and Jesse have studied the cultures of people with a specific interest in the role of sports. By delivering new perspectives on sports history, Brett and Jesse have a knack for reigniting the feelings fans get when witnessing sporting events.

Jesse Matlock
C • Wheatland Huskies

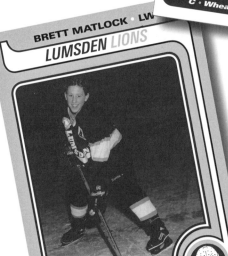

BRETT MATLOCK • LW
LUMSDEN *LIONS*